"If God has called you to minister t(
Women's Ministry not only helps y
gives you the tools needed to create
fall in love with Jesus and truly supp.... .... This is the resource I've
been looking for as a pastor's wife and ministry leader – I highly, highly
recommend!"

—**Joanna Weaver,** best-selling author, *Having a Mary Heart in a Martha World*

"With the demise of women's ministry, Cyndee's book should be required
reading for *every* leader in our church today. And I don't just mean women
leaders. *All pastors*, please read this book so you know how to serve the
women in your church. Our churches are leaving a huge hole because the
women have been left behind and have nowhere to turn. This is a much-
needed resource for the church today. "

—**Shari Braendel,** founder of Fashion Meets Faith and author
of *Help Me, Jesus, I Have Nothing to Wear!* (Zondervan)

"A must-read for anyone leading or serving in women's ministry. Lead an
established ministry that needs refreshing? Check. Starting from scratch?
Check. Hosting inside your church? Check. In your neighborhood? Check.
Cyndee Ownbey shares decades of leadership knowledge that will encourage
and empower you to rethink the ministry God has placed in your hands."

—**Kristin Schell,** author *The Turquoise Table: Finding Community and
Connection in Your Own Front Yard*

"Cyndee Ownbey has thought of every impactful detail when it comes to
serving women to love Jesus, their families, and others well through the
local church body ... a must-read, and a resource for every ministry leader.
She walks you through all the details to usher in a space for the Spirit to
move and bring unity among His people."

—**Jessi Strother,** speaker, writer, friend, and founder
of the women's ministry Salty, Sweet

"This book is a definite must-have for anyone in women's ministry
leadership! Cyndee speaks from the heart and with years of experience,
which makes the information invaluable. I can't recommend this book
highly enough!"

—**Kristi Bomar,** women's ministry coordinator, Faith
Outreach Christian Center - Navasota, TX

"If you're a women's ministry leader, *Rethinking Women's Ministry* is your
essential handbook! Author Cyndee Ownbey asks the right questions,
provides practical solutions, then directs leaders to seek God for how their
ministry can best glorify Him. You can trust Cyndee's twenty years of
experience to guide your ministry to the next level."

—**Leslie Bennett,** manager of women's ministry initiatives, Revive Our Hearts

"*Rethinking Women's Ministry* is a must for any woman involved with women's ministry or any ministry. Cyndee offers a wealth of timeless and practical wisdom and tools from her over twenty years serving and leading in women's ministry. What I love most about this book is the emphasis on community, authentic relationships, Biblical literacy, and the importance of Bible teachers receiving solid training and Bible education."

—**Erin Bishop,** founder/president, Whatever Girls

"Cyndee's book gives much-needed focus. Never losing sight of the goal of pointing women to Christ, and helping them dig into God's Word, she gives rich, practical help to those in women's ministry ... She roots us in the "why" behind the work, and lays out the intentional "how" to do women's ministry in a way that keeps our eyes on the goal. I want to put this in the hands of every women's ministry leader I know."

—**Gretchen Ronnevik,** women's ministry leader and founder of Gospel Mentoring

"Cyndee Ownbey challenges us to take a fresh look at our women's ministry framework—to authentically consider what is going well and what isn't. Passionate about encouraging and equipping women leaders, Cyndee lovingly uncovers our assumptions, traditions, motivations, and so much more as she leads us into an examination of who it is we're really serving, and how to connect with them. Cyndee's practical and actionable tips and ideas will help us find, unite, and equip our women!"

—**Jo Ann Fore,** community manager, Women Leading Women, author, *When a Woman Finds Her Voice*

"*Rethinking Women's Ministry* is a breath of fresh air that every women's ministry leader needs to have on her bookshelf. I've been in women's ministry for almost fifteen years and have never seen a more valuable resource than Cyndee's book. She covers every area of women's ministry and the struggles we face in our current church culture with grace and gives specific ideas for improvement and change. Her experience and creativity along with her down-to-earth personality give readers tangible takeaways and a clear plan for what to do next."

—**Micah Maddox,** pastor's wife, speaker, and author of *Anchored In: Experience a Power-Full Life in a Problem-Filled World*

"*Rethinking Women's Ministry* is the consummate, complete companion for any women's ministry leader. Cyndee asks *and* answers the hard questions about this important ministry of the church. She draws her wisdom from a wealth of experience from leading women's ministry. Her honest and practical guidance along with assessment tools and good solutions makes this book a must-read."

—**Gina Duke,** award-winning author, *Organizing Your Prayer Closet*, former director of women's ministry, First Baptist, Portland, TN

ReTHINKING
WOMEN'S MINISTRY

biblical, practical tools
for *cultivating* a
flourishing community

Cyndee Ownbey

Jill,
may you seek
the Lord in
all you do!
Cyndee
Prov 3:5-6

ONB
PRESS

Cover design and page design by Michelle Rayburn.
www.missionandmedia.com

Copy edit by Michelle Rayburn.

ISBN-13: 978-1-7334710-0-8

Printed in the United States of America

Contents

PART 3
Implementing Change

About This Book

The following pages contain stories gleaned from my experiences in ministering to women for more than twenty years. God has given me the opportunity to serve and actively participate in women's ministries in five different churches. I served in a variety of church sizes, different denominations, and in single and multiple campuses. I have a lot of stories to share, many highlighting the mistakes I've made and the lessons I've learned.

I'm not only sharing personal stories, but also those of thousands of leaders collected through online surveys, emails, and Facebook. While not every example shared may apply to your specific situation, I pray there will be pieces you'll find applicable.

I treasure the opportunity to come alongside you and cheer you on as you serve and seek God's will for your ministry. May the Lord abundantly bless your efforts to cultivate a flourishing women's ministry in your church and community!

HOW TO USE THIS BOOK

You'll soon discover that I'm a rather practical woman. Like the women who attend your women's ministry events, I'm always asking, "What's in it for me?" I have a lot of items on my to-do list, and to be brutally honest, I don't like to waste time. I don't want to waste yours either.

As you read through this book, I want to suggest that you make note of two things:

1. Prayer Points: As you sense God giving you a little nudge (or a big nudge), write the letters "PP" beside that sentence or section. That will be your cue to make that idea or thought a matter of prayer.

2. Action Items: There may be ideas or tips that you know without a doubt your team needs to implement immediately. Most likely, they'll be small tweaks that you may have already considered but haven't put into practice. Mark those items with the letters "AI."

At the end of each chapter, there will be a space for you to capture your Prayer Points and Action Items so you won't have to flip through every page. Consider turning down the page corner or adding a sticky note (for fellow type-A girls) for easy reference.

Lord, I ask You to give each leader discernment and vision as they journey through these pages. I know You have great plans for "your girls" and the ministries they oversee. Guide and direct their efforts as they seek to point their women to Your Word and to the hope that can only be found in a relationship with You. Amen.

Bonus Materials

You'll find the worksheets, forms, and assessments mentioned throughout *Rethinking Women's Ministry* available as a free downloadable PDF at: **www.rethinkingwomensministry.com**.

Introduction

"Why aren't women coming to women's ministry events?" It's the heart cry I hear on a weekly basis from women's ministry leaders. Leaders long to know what they can do to encourage women to show up. Some know they need to make changes, but they aren't sure what those changes should be. Other leaders are frustrated with team members who won't budge because "this is the way we've always done it."

The face of women's ministry is changing, and many women's ministry teams – perhaps even your own – have struggled to adapt. Twenty years ago God called me to join Him in this journey to minister to women. Much of what worked really well twenty years ago doesn't garner the same robust results now.

Rethinking Women's Ministry is designed to help women's ministry leaders and team members examine what is working well in their church ministry and what isn't. We'll start by looking at how things have changed over the years. What's really different? What new challenges must we tackle? Then we'll move on to the heart of the matter – identifying areas where change is needed. Do you need to rethink your team structure, Bible studies, or discipleship approach? Does your event framework, outreach, or publicity need to be refreshed? As God highlights areas that need rethinking, you'll be able to form an action plan that will enable your ministry to reach more women more effectively and create a community that flourishes.

You'll also hear what women really think about women's ministry events and activities as I share statistics and comments gathered from 1,140 women in an online survey.[1] Some of their comments even surprised me!

Like me, you may be anxious to get started – there are women to reach! Before we jump knee deep into the need for rethinking women's ministry, we need to agree upon a definition. What is women's ministry?

I posed this question to women's ministry leaders in our Women's Ministry Toolbox Community group on Facebook. Here's how they defined women's ministry:

> *"A privilege assigned by our almighty God to grow in faith together."*

> *"A ministry that serves the spiritual (discipleship, teaching, training), emotional (mentoring, encouraging, fellowship, counseling), and physical (comforting, provision, helping) needs of women."*

> *"We, as the leaders, minister, encourage, equip, build confidence, and support the women of our church who then go out, reach other women, and bring them back to the church where the process starts over again."*

> *"Women ministering to women in the context of the church, in alignment with the vision of the church, in submission to the leadership of the church. The ministry exists to equip, connect, comfort, and grow women and help them live out their mission as necessary and essential partners in fulfilling the great commission."*

> *"To help women grow in their relationship with God and with others."*

> *"Amazing. Complicated. Fulfilling. Exhausting. Peaceful. Dramatic. Crazy. But worthwhile."*

Search the Scriptures all you want, but you won't find a formal organization of a ministry for women. But God doesn't leave us without some guidelines. We are told in Titus 2:3-5 that the older women are to teach the younger women. We are also told in Acts 2:42 that the early church "devoted themselves to the apostles' teaching, to the fellowship, to the breaking of bread, and to prayer" (CSB). In Matthew 28:19, we are instructed to go and make disciples (all of us). There are additional "one anothers" scattered throughout Scripture: love one another (John 13:14), encourage one another (Hebrews 3:13), serve one another (Galatians 5:13), tell one another about God (Psalm 145:4), carry one another's burdens (Galatians 6:2).

We can say with confidence that biblical instruction, older women teaching younger women, discipleship, fellowship, and prayer *should* happen! Service, love, encouragement, sharing the gospel, and carrying burdens round out our responsibilities to one another.

I've boiled it down to this:

> Women's ministry is an arm of the church that intentionally provides biblically sound encouragement and spiritually driven growth opportunities for all women.

You may have a different definition. You may even have a purpose statement for your women's ministry that serves as a guideline for everything you do. If you don't have a working definition of a women's ministry for your team, may I suggest that you spend time creating one? You're welcome to use mine or tweak it a bit to make it your own. Seek input from your pastoral staff so they can hold your team accountable.

Here's the thing – we can't hit a target if we don't know what we're aiming for. Let's get started!

PART 1
Shifting Target Audience

See, I am doing a new thing! Now it springs up; do you not perceive it? I am making a way in the wilderness and streams in the wasteland.
—Isaiah 43:19

Chapter 1

Who Are We Trying to Reach?

"Therefore go and make disciples of all nations, baptizing them in the name of the Father and of the Son and of the Holy Spirit, and teaching them to obey everything I have commanded you. And surely I am with you always, to the very end of the age."
—Matthew 28:19-20

THE STRUGGLE IS REAL. LOW ATTENDANCE, generation gaps, volunteer droughts, and disinterest grieve the hearts of many ministry leaders. My heart breaks alongside theirs as more and more women dismiss the heart work and hard work of women's ministry teams on their behalf. Teams desperate to drive up attendance pull out all the stops – big-name speakers, beautiful and elaborate décor, handmade favors, remarkable door prizes, and countless hours of preparation – all in hopes of showering their women with the love of Christ. Yet our efforts are often met with lackluster enthusiasm, flimsy excuses, and minimal commitment.

"I might be able to come."

"I think we have something that day."

"It's not really my thing."

We're left wondering, *What's keeping our women from participating*? Is there anything we can do to change things? If we need to change something, what do we need to change? Will anything we do even make a difference?

Throughout this book, I am going to ask you to rethink ideas, events, and practices that have quite possibly become the norm in your church. People often joke that the definition of insanity is doing the same thing over and over again, expecting different results. Please know, I'm not calling you or your team insane, but I do believe that to change the outcome, we need to employ different tactics.

THE FIRST STEP

The first step in rethinking women's ministry is a generational examination. We need to educate ourselves on the generational norms of the women we have been tasked to reach (those inside and outside the church). Entire books have been written on generational differences. For now, our focus will be on millennials (born between 1980 and 2000) and Generation Z (born between 1999 and 2015). A side note here: The overlap is intentional; those on the fringe may fall into either category. Millennials are often unengaged in women's ministry, and our older Gen Z women are just dipping their toes into the women's ministry pool.

To change the outcome, we need to employ different tactics.

According to Thom and Jess Rainer in *The Millennials: Connecting to America's Largest Generation*, millennials want to serve, make a difference, and contribute to the world. They are marrying much later in life and are committed to marrying just once or not at all. The average age of a woman's first marriage is 25.5, but 65% are cohabitating at least once before marriage. Most see nothing wrong with same-sex marriage. They are attached to their parents, regularly seeking their advice. If they have children of their own, they strive to be an involved parent. Millennials are not regular church attenders. Three out of four label themselves as spiritual but not religious. They struggle to define what they believe. They are teachable and long to have mentors that will come alongside them and listen. Diversity is a non-issue; it is their reality. Relationships are a key motivator for this generation.

Christian millennials are devoted to Bible study and prayer, and they long to reach and minister to people in the community.[2]

Barna Group defines Gen Z as the largest, most ethnically and racially diverse American generation yet. More than half use screen media for four or more hours each day, earning them the nickname "screenagers." They view social media as a place to find information, discuss topics, and manicure their online presence. They are sensitive to the feelings and experiences of others, but wary of categorizing any view as right or wrong. Most are confused and uncertain about what is true. One third say gender is how a person feels inside. While teen pregnancies have decreased, the rates of suicide and depression have skyrocketed for this group of young people. They are focused on personal happiness and financial success. They were not born into a Christian culture, and only 4% claim to have a biblical worldview. Many are a spiritual blank slate.[3]

I share those fast facts not to discourage you but to inform you. Church attendance is no longer the cultural norm. To ignore the issues and challenges our women face would be a mistake.

As the authors point out in *Gen Z*, "When a missionary immerses herself in a culture different from her own, she doesn't expect the people who live there to speak and act and think like people from home – in fact, she expects quite the opposite: that *she* will have to change in order to connect with people."[4]

If we want to connect with the women from the millennial and Gen Z generations, we're probably going to need to make some changes.

THE SECOND STEP

The second step in rethinking women's ministry requires acknowledging the current barriers to our women's participation. If you've been serving in women's ministry for a few years, you've likely noticed a decline in the number of women in attendance or at least the number of active women in certain age groups. You may be eager for tips and ideas to overcome your low participation numbers. Before you jump ahead to another chapter, I want to encourage you to consider the following barriers so you can best respond to them.

CURRENT BARRIERS TO PARTICIPATION

Which of these may be a barrier to the women in your church?

Work – Historically, stay-at-home moms were the primary target audience for women's ministry. Ministries often revolved around daytime Bible studies and mommy groups. If you've noticed dwindling numbers over the years, that's no mistake. According to the Women's Bureau, a unit of the U.S. Department of Labor, a 2017 report says 70% of mothers who have children under age eighteen participate in the labor force, and of those mothers, over 75% are employed full time.[5] If most of our activities are still aimed at the stay-at-home mom or only offered during the workday, no wonder attendance has dropped! It's also interesting to note that "mothers are the primary or sole wage earners for 40% of households with children under age eighteen today, as compared with 11% in 1960."[6] Targeting traditional stay-at-home moms and retirees is no longer an effective strategy. We're reaching the minority, instead of the majority.

Do you know how many of your women work? Do you know when they work? Survey your women to gain a better understanding of your target audience. Find out if they work, how many hours they work, and when they work.

It is vital to acknowledge the current barriers to our women's participation.

We'll discuss strategies in later chapters to address working women's schedules and needs.

Spiritual apathy – Weekly church attendance that was once a cultural norm is now the exception, not the rule. According to Thom S. Rainer, twenty years ago "a church member was considered active in the church if he or she attended three times a week. Today, a church member is considered active in the church if he or she attends three times a month."[7]

We exist in what has been labeled a "post-Christian era." The influence of the church and Christianity is diminishing. Research reveals a steady decline in each generation of the percentage of people who hold a biblical worldview. According to Barna Group, 10% of boomers, 7% of Generation X, and 6% of millennials have a biblical worldview; this is compared to only 4% of Generation Z that have a biblical worldview.[8]

Rather than view this as a crisis, we can embrace it as an opportunity and change our tactics accordingly. In the pages that follow, you'll find many ideas for reaching women who appear to be apathetic about church and religion.

Biblical illiteracy – This barrier, which we're probably most likely to dismiss, is a large problem inside of and outside of our churches. LifeWay Research found that about half of Americans (53%) have read "relatively little of the Bible." One out of ten people has read none of it, while 13% say they have read a few sentences. The study reports that 30% "say they have read several passages or stories."[9]

Despite regular attendance at Sunday services, Bible study, or even vacation Bible school as a child, the depth of biblical knowledge of our members is lacking. They do not know or understand what Scripture teaches about being in community with other believers, serving others, and engaging in discipleship. They may never have been taught about the importance of spiritual disciplines and practices, so it follows that there is little desire for, or priority given to, women's ministry events.

Family – While we might typically expect a child's sporting event to trump a scheduled women's ministry event, lately, sports practices, musical lessons, and club meetings have been elevated to the same level of importance. Guilt, fear of missing out (FOMO), and peer pressure encourage women to always be present. Family time has become a treasured and protected commodity as husbands work longer hours and moms juggle working too. Family outings will almost always trump women's ministry as well.

It isn't just the women with young families that feel the pull; women with aging parents are often the primary caregivers. Women in these situations find themselves giving unconditionally of their time and resources with little time or energy left over for women's ministry events or activities.

Cliques – Women's ministry has rightly earned the reputation of being "cliquey." Women love to sit and visit with their friends, often to the exclusion of others in the room. Holy huddles are commonplace. Inside jokes leave the new girl in the dark. Even our volunteer teams draw women from the same pool. Our use of Christianese language leaves new believers and unbelievers on the outside.

Beyond our women gathering in tight-knit groups, our presentations and discussion questions are often directed toward a core group of women. One woman who I surveyed pointed out that meetings and events are "directed primarily at moms" or they assume "a homogenous audience, with similar interests, outlooks, culture, and calling." By excluding the experiences of other women, we create cliques!

You'll find many clique-busting tips in the pages to come.

Cultural –The glance at millennials and Gen Z at the beginning of this chapter hints to the great need for biblical truth. The world and the church offer very different views on sexuality, abortion, truth, gender, and purpose. Messages preached from the pulpit often stand in direct opposition to what the world and public schools are preaching. And social media has changed the way we discover and share information.

We'll engage the culture head-on as we rethink the types and topics of women's ministry events God may be directing us to host.

As we've seen in our quick examination of generational tendencies, the women we seek to serve today are quite different from those that women's ministry served even twenty years ago. Our target audience has shifted and continues to shift. What worked in years past may not work in its current form today. If we want to reach more women and reach women more effectively, we need to be willing to rethink our approach.

Prayer

Lord, help us to open our eyes to see the women in our church and community as they are. Help us to be more aware of where they sit spiritually. Loosen our grip on how we've carried out women's ministry events in the past and show us how we specifically need to rethink and tweak our ministry to better reach the women You've placed in our path. Amen.

PRAYER POINTS: WHAT IS GOD PROMPTING ME TO MAKE A MATTER OF PRAYER?

PP

_____
_____
_____
_____
_____
_____
_____

ACTION ITEMS: LIST THOSE THINGS UPON WHICH YOU SENSE GOD IS PROMPTING YOU TO TAKE ACTION.

AI

_____
_____
_____
_____
_____
_____
_____

Chapter 2

Impact of Social Media and the Internet

"Everything is permissible," but not everything is beneficial.
"Everything is permissible," but not everything builds up.
—1 Corinthians 10:23 CSB

OUR DISCUSSION ON BARRIERS TO PARTICIPATION would not be complete without addressing advances in technology, social media, and the internet, so let's talk about it up front. The introduction of the first iPhone in 2007 has had a profound impact on how we connect with one another and access information. Admittedly, leaders twenty years ago didn't have to compete with online ministries, smartphones, blogs, or social media. Every day the competition between the physical church and the online world increases.

In this chapter, we'll examine why women are leaving the local church and flocking to online ministries, and we'll discuss ways the internet undermines our ministry efforts.

But first, let's get a big-picture look at the way we use and interact with social media and the internet. Statistics reveal rather startling facts.

- American adults spend over eleven hours per day listening to, watching, reading, or generally interacting with media.[10]

- Almost half of women ages eighteen to thirty-four check their phones as soon as they wake up, and another 36% check them within five minutes.[11]
- Eighty-eight percent of women said they compare themselves to images in the media, with half saying the comparison is unfavorable.[12]
- Sixty percent of women from all age groups said they wouldn't post a photo of themselves on social media unless they loved the way they looked.[13]
- Roughly two-thirds of U.S. adults (68%) now report that they are Facebook users, and roughly three-quarters of those users access Facebook on a daily basis.[14]

We cannot ignore the presence and impact of technology, social media, and the internet on the lives of the women we seek to reach. We'll talk in later chapters about how we can use technology for good, including using it to build community and publicize events. For now, I want to walk through some of the challenges and negative effects of technology on women's ministries.

WHY WOMEN ARE LEAVING THE LOCAL CHURCH AND FLOCKING TO ONLINE MINISTRIES

Only in the last five to ten years have church-based women's ministry teams had to compete with online women's ministries. Across the country and around the world, women are leaving their local church and joining online Christian communities in large numbers. While we struggle to attract women to women's ministry events, online ministries for women are flourishing.

Why are women leaving the physical church and heading online? And how do we stop this mass exodus? We need to look at the reasons why women are leaving, address them, and make any needed changes so women aren't running away from, but to the local church.

Here are seven reasons why women are leaving the physical church for online ministry and how we can make changes to stop the exodus:

IMPACT OF SOCIAL MEDIA AND THE INTERNET | **25**

1. Women have been hurt by church members.

Problem: Whether it is an issue of gossip, a snarky attitude, hypocrisy, or some kind of snub, wounded women are seeking safe places.

Solution: We must lead by example, and teach our women to love one another, offer forgiveness, and seek restoration.

2. Freedom from conviction.

Problem: Online interactions allow women to pick and choose what they share. Don't want someone to see that sin you're struggling with? Hide it. If they want to have their ears tickled with partial, omitted, or twisted Scripture, it's there for the taking. In *#Struggles: Following Jesus in a Selfie-Centered World*, Craig Groeschel points out, "Our modern ability to manage our image encourages and makes it easier for us to wear veils that cover up the truth."[15]

Solution: We allow the Holy Spirit to convict. We need to take off our veils and openly share our faults and struggles. When God prompts us to confront (and only then), we do so in the most loving way possible (never publicly). It's important to teach our women the whole truth of God's Word.

3. Efforts to serve or lead have been rebuffed.

Problem: Many women are eager to serve and even lead, but churches and women's ministries often make it difficult to become involved. Opportunities aren't vocalized, volunteer training is lacking, the path into leadership is unclear, and the desire for control is so strong that others are intentionally locked out.

Solution: When a woman volunteers, say yes and put her to work as soon as possible. Offer regular training for all of your volunteer roles. Encourage your team to reach out into the church and outside of their circle of friends as they recruit volunteers. Explain the process and qualifications for leadership roles and help women find places where they can serve.

4. Condemnation for a committed or perceived sin.

Problem: Churches can be ruthless when it comes to offering grace and restoration. Divorced? You may be shunned. Had an abortion? You may be shamed. Struggle with a mental illness? You're not praying hard enough. Had an affair? You need to leave.

Solution: Let's put a stop to slapping labels on one another. Let's not tolerate gossip of any kind. Let's ask God to help us to see past the outer actions to the heart of our women. Let's resolve to never belittle, condemn, or even joke about an area with which one of our women may be struggling. Let's love them where they are, pray for God to bring awareness, and help them (when asked) to overcome their stumbling blocks.

Let's love them where they are, pray for God to bring awareness, and help them (when asked) to overcome their stumbling blocks.

5. Little or no time to share.

Problem: Many women want to talk. They want to share what's going on in their lives, and they want to talk about what they are learning. Online that is easy to do. In real life many of our women's ministry events are structured like a college lecture. If there's a discussion time, it's usually relegated to the end and is often cut short.

Solution: Build your events *around* discussion. Set up tables with chairs instead of rows. Prepare questions in advance. Train discussion group and table leaders to keep the conversation moving and on topic while following the leading of the Holy Spirit. Challenge your women with application questions. If you're going to have a speaker, request discussion questions and plan time for the women to talk through what they have just heard and learned. Discussions help solidify the information they've just received.

6. Seeking specific help.

Problem: Your church doesn't offer a ministry that caters to their specific need or situation – step-parenting, divorce, abortion, depression, autism, widowhood, single parenting, married to an unbeliever, caring for aging parents, going through cancer, etc.

Solution: Partner with other churches or organizations in your area. Find out if DivorceCare or Celebrate Recovery offers a chapter meeting in your area. Know what ministries you can refer women to so they can receive in-person mentoring and support. If there's a big need in your church, then speak with your pastoral staff about launching a ministry to address those needs.

7. Convenience.

Problem: Women want resources, Bible studies, and events that work with their schedule. They want to jump in now, rather than wait for the next women's ministry event or the start of the next Bible study session. Some of your women have to wait *months* to get plugged in.

Solution: We need to keep the door open and the lights on. Look for ways you can plug women in quickly! Do you need to add more meetings to your calendar? Let women come to Bible study even if there's only a week or two left. God will use the time they do have with your women to build relationships. Make it known that women are welcome to join at any time.

∽

Please hear my heart on this; I'm not saying all online ministry is bad. Many Christ-focused online ministries can meet the needs of women when our church and team are not able. A woman may need resources that only a community that understands her needs can provide, such as navigating a rare or chronic medical diagnosis. The local church should be the first responders – arriving in person on the scene the moment crisis hits. If our local church and area ministries are unable to provide assistance, then we may need to refer our women to biblically sound online resources.

Lord, we ask You to reveal the things our church and ministry may be doing that keep our women away. Help us to be a safe haven for the hurting. May every woman who comes to our events feel valued and loved. Amen.

4 Ways the Internet Undermines our Ministry Efforts

I am amazed by all of the resources that have popped up on the internet over the last ten years. Need an icebreaker idea? Google it. Want to know what the Bible says about a topic? Search for it. Looking for an event idea? Pinterest is your happy place. I've been guilty of putting Google before God, and I'm guessing you have too. The internet provides another place for Satan to distract us and set traps for us to fall into.

Four internet traps to avoid:

1. The internet undermines our ministry when we listen to online authorities and bloggers instead of God. (And yes, this includes me.)

Browse around the internet long enough, and you'll find conflicting information on almost every topic, including women's ministry and Scripture. We must constantly check the advice we receive and teaching we hear against God's Word. We need to learn to ignore those things that stand in opposition to the direction God has given us.

2. We get our direction from Pinterest (or websites) instead of seeking God's direction for our events, themes, and Bible studies.

I get a lot of emails from leaders asking for a list of event themes, and I kindly respond that I purposefully don't have one. I follow up with a plea to spend time in prayer and God's Word seeking what God wants for their specific group of women.

3. We are discouraged when we compare our numbers, our décor, and our budget with others.

Social media gives us a glimpse of events at other churches that feature big-name speakers, gorgeous flower arrangements, extravagant retreat locations, and hand-crafted event favors that lead us to feel the need to step up our game big time. We stress ourselves, our team, and our budget as we struggle to keep up with the church on the other side of the screen. We need to remember that every ministry situation is unique, and large budgets and big turnouts don't dictate or indicate spiritual growth or salvation.

4. Satan plants seeds of doubt. We can leave our team meeting confident in the direction God has led our team only to open a new email or web page to be bombarded by a thought or idea that causes us to question the decisions we just made.

☙

When we spend time "Googling" and "pinning" and not on our faces and in His Word, we lose focus on God's message for our women and His plan for our ministry. We become trapped in the cycle of comparison and disappointed if our efforts don't measure up. Instead, may we yield to the teaching in Matthew 6:33, which says, "But seek first the kingdom of God and his righteousness, and all these things will be added to you" (ESV).

Prayer

Father, God, I ask You to give each one of us discernment as we sift through women's ministry ideas on the internet. Help us to not be fearful of what is available online, but to seek out that which can be used to further Your kingdom. May the ideas we choose to use never undermine Your plans for the women in our church and community. Help us to seek You first, above all else. In Jesus's name, I pray, Amen.

PRAYER POINTS: WHAT IS GOD PROMPTING ME TO MAKE A MATTER OF PRAYER?

PP

_____

_____

_____

_____

_____

_____

_____

ACTION ITEMS: LIST THOSE THINGS UPON WHICH YOU SENSE GOD IS PROMPTING YOU TO TAKE ACTION.

AI

_____

_____

_____

_____

_____

_____

_____

Chapter 3

Community
and Cliques

*And let us consider how we may spur one another on toward
love and good deeds, not giving up meeting together, as
some are in the habit of doing, but encouraging one another
- and all the more as you see the Day approaching.*
—Hebrews 10:24–25

YOU KNOW THOSE WORD ASSOCIATION GAMES where one person says a word and then the other person says the first word that comes to mind? If we were to play that game with the women in your church, how would they respond when you say "women's ministry"? Would the word "cliques" come to mind?

In the women I surveyed, the number two complaint about women's ministry events – behind lack of depth – was cliques. Cliques are unfortunately common in churches and especially so in women's ministry. Whenever a group of women gathers together, smaller groups are bound to form. As leaders, we want to see our women bond and new relationships form. But when those groups of women become, as defined by the Oxford Dictionary, "a small group of people, with shared interests or other features in common, who spend time together and *do not readily allow others to join them*" (italics mine),[16] then we have a problem.

So how do we cultivate community without creating cliques? In this chapter, you'll find many ideas that will encourage your women to grow in the relationships with one another. We'll look at what it's like to be the new girl in the room. We'll walk through some ways your team can intentionally create opportunities for connection and community. The most successful ministries will implement a multi-pronged approach delivered with love and consistency.

While only God can change the hearts of our women, we can plant seeds, encourage diversity, and issue frequent reminders.

If cliques have become a stronghold in your ministry, be prepared for some pushback. Some of your women are happy and content with their clique and will see no need to change things up. I've heard countless stories of women who refused to follow directions and raised a stink when they were asked to separate from their friends. From tears to outright defiance, there's a much deeper heart issue at play here. Changing the culture is going to take time, prayer, and the Holy Spirit. While only God can change the hearts of our women, we can plant seeds, encourage diversity, and issue frequent reminders.

WE WERE CREATED FOR COMMUNITY

God has wired us for community. From the very beginning in the garden, God placed us in community with Himself and with one another. "The LORD God said, 'It is not good for the man to be alone. I will make a helper suitable for him'" (Genesis 2:18). God never intended for us to be alone. We are better together. As Pastor Robby Gallaty points out, "We weren't created for solitude, but rather for deeply connected, intentionally accountable community that legitimately looks out for and works with one another."[17]

Some of our women have lived without community for so long that they have forgotten its importance. Other women have replaced face-to-face community with online community and have neglected the instructions in God's Word to meet together, worship together, and learn together with other believers (see Hebrews 10:24–25). It's quite likely you'll need to set a good example and create places and spaces for them to experience community with one another, praying that over time women will see the beauty and benefits of Christian community.

Ways to Quickly Build Community

Let's dive into nine practical ways in which your team can build community.

1. Pray for Community

I placed this in the number one spot intentionally. Before we do anything, we should ask God to move on the hearts of our women. Pray for a greater concern for one another, sweet times of sharing, the breaking apart of cliques, and new friendships to form. Spend time personally and as a team praying for God to unify your women. 2 Corinthians 13:11 is a great starting point, "Finally, brothers and sisters, rejoice! Strive for full restoration, encourage one another, be of one mind, live in peace. And the God of love and peace will be with you." You may also want to pray Colossians 3:14, 1 Corinthians 1:10, 1 Peter 3:8, and Ephesians 4:1-6.

2. Intentional Icebreakers

Before you or the women on your team roll your eyes, hear me out. I'm not talking about silly icebreaker games. Intentional icebreakers can provide quick points of connection when they highlight shared experiences and personal preferences. You can bet when Tammy discovers that Alma has traveled to Greece, her dream vacation destination, she'll continue that conversation later. Consider games that require women to circulate around the room and talk with others. Surface-level, getting-to-know-you questions set the stage for going deeper. Check the resource list at the back of the book for icebreaker games that will cultivate community.

Intentional icebreakers can provide quick points of connection when they highlight shared experiences and personal preferences.

3. Seating Arrangements

Most leaders bristle when I mention assigned seating, and I admit, I had to be sold on the idea too. The church we currently attend frequently uses assigned seating at women's ministry events and even at some church events. Assigned seating is expected. Church leaders are intentional about placing people who do not know one another together and separating cliques. Seating arrangements are always created prayerfully and with grace, making sure that women who bring guests are always seated together. Sometimes we are seated based on the area of town in which we live. Table leaders are tasked with helping to facilitate the discussion and usually use icebreaker questions to launch the conversation.

Rows send a signal to your women that they are about to receive a lecture. Most women I know aren't coming to a women's event to be talked to; they are coming to talk with others. Physically changing the direction the chairs face communicates:

- The person on the stage is not the focus.
- The women sitting next to you desire and deserve your attention.
- We're going to give you time to talk to one another.
- This is about "us" not about "you" and "me."

Depending upon your space constraints and numbers, you may need to have your women sit in rows to listen to your speaker. Get them out of those rows and into circles (with or without tables) soon after the speaker finishes so they can have a great discussion. There's something very impersonal about sitting in the back of the room looking toward the stage over row after row of the back of women's heads. As the pastor over small groups at my church says, "Life is better in circles."

Assigned seating is a great way to ensure women from multiple generations interact with each other. And assigned seating removes that awkward "where do I sit?" dilemma.

4. Name Tags

Yes, I know this sounds so basic, but I can't tell you how many times name tags are forgotten, or leaders think they are no longer needed. Being able to call someone by name builds connection and community. Help out your sisters who struggle to remember names by using name tags at every event or activity. Use printed name tags when possible so names are both legible and large enough to be read from across the table or the circle.

5. Discussion Groups

Discussion groups aren't just for Bible studies. Provide discussion questions for your women to answer after any speaker or teaching. Allow women to process and share what your speaker has discussed. Your women will grow in relationship with one another when they share their answers.

Discussion group guidelines (available in the free bonus materials online) create a safe space where women can share without fear of gossip or judgment. I suggest reading your guidelines out loud to the group. If your group will repeatedly meet – over a retreat weekend or as a weekly Bible study – have the group sign and return the guidelines and then hold women accountable if they struggle or fail to uphold them.

6. Regular Gatherings

Community builds over time. There's no way around it! The more opportunities we provide for women to connect, the more connected our women can be. Pray about how your team can provide consistent opportunities for women to connect.

7. Multi-Day Events

A larger chunk of time together will expedite community building too! Conferences, mission trips, and retreats that offer extended, focused time away from home provide multiple opportunities for connection and deepening relationships. The shared experiences – the speaker, the small group discussions, the meals, the late-night games, the service projects – will bond your women together.

8. Share Prayer Requests

Now we're building community, not fear – so hear me out on this one. The most nonthreatening way I know of to share prayer requests and build community is to have women write two or three personal prayer requests on a notecard and have them trade with a person at their table or in their group. For example, ask everyone to pass their card to the right. I beg you, please, please don't have everyone hold hands and stand in a circle. Holding hands, even if it happens to be someone you know, can be extremely awkward for some of your women. For some it's too intimate a gesture, for others it provides a distraction from the prayer time. *Are my hands sweaty? I hope I don't catch her cold. How much longer are we going to stand here?* Save those prayer circles for times when you pray with your closest friends.

Prayer softens hearts and opens the door for deeper relationships and creates an intimacy that stretches beyond that moment.

It's much more difficult to be catty with someone you've prayed for and who has prayed over you. Prayer softens hearts and opens the door for deeper relationships and creates an intimacy that stretches beyond that moment.

9. Introductions

I always write this on my agenda because it's so easy to forget! Make introductions more memorable (and increase points of connection) by asking everyone to share their answer to a quick (not deep) icebreaker question. "31 Introduction Icebreaker Questions" is included in the free bonus materials online.

WHEN WOMEN RESIST EFFORTS TO BUILD COMMUNITY

Our Bible study coordinator looked me square in the eyes and told me that if I wanted to assign women to discussion groups, I would need to be the one to do it. She went on to share about a situation several years earlier in which a couple of women flat out refused to attend their assigned discussion groups because they did not want to be separated. Each week, as she would announce it was time to divide up into groups, these two women would slip off together to the same group. Gentle reminders to attend their assigned groups were met with tears and then hostility. Still nursing deep wounds, she had zero desire to get into a battle with anyone ever again over Bible study group assignments.

As the new girl on the team, I decided to use that to my advantage. I didn't have a history with these women, and to their knowledge, I had no idea what issues had come up with Bible study groups in the past. I was prepared for a bit of pushback but prayed it wouldn't happen. At our intro week of Bible study that fall, I shared with our group of about thirty-five women that we would be dividing them up into three smaller groups. We asked each one to fill out an information card noting their decade (twenties, thirties, forties, fifties, sixties, etc.) on the top right corner of their card. I explained that after our time together, our group leaders would meet. We were going to pray over the cards and ask the Lord to arrange our groups. I shared with them how God had repeatedly placed me in just the right Bible study group without fail. Knowing how anxious some of them would be, we promised to have their group leader email them promptly.

When we formed our Bible study groups later that morning:

- We coupled the cards of church members with the guest they had invited to the study so they would be assigned to the same group.
- We divided our cards into piles by decades so we could form multi-generational groups.
- We shuffled each pile of cards and flipped them upside down so we couldn't see the names.
- We prayed and asked the Lord to place our women where He wanted them.
- Our group leaders each took turns drawing one card from a pile until no cards remained, moving to the next decade as

needed. Our goal was to balance the groups so that all ages were represented as equally as possible.

- Once all the cards had been distributed, each group leader flipped her cards over and prayerfully examined her group. If there was a known conflict (ex-wife and current wife or other situation that might cause division), then we adjusted the groups. We tried very hard not to alter the groups the Lord created unless we all agreed it was necessary.

I have no doubt some of our women were disappointed they were in a different group from one or more of their friends, but they were welcome to socialize before class, sit together during our opening, and could visit again after our discussion group time. At the end of the study, we had many comments from our women on our survey that they loved having a wide variety of ages in their group. In time, they realized, as Sophie Hudson describes in *Giddy Up, Eunice: Because Women Need Each Other*, "We can find comfort and encouragement from someone in similar circumstances even if we don't belong to the same demographic."[18]

While I pray your efforts to cultivate community are received warmly by the women in your church, I know that's not always the case. Don't let a few grumbles or groans keep you from moving forward with plans to bust up cliques. Refuse to participate in or tolerate poor behavior. You may have to pull another woman aside to lovingly discuss her behavior. Assume she wasn't aware and pray for her. If a one-on-one meeting doesn't yield results, I encourage you to seek godly counsel. A meeting with your pastor may be necessary and can help you determine the best way to manage that specific situation.

Over time, most will tire of instigating or complaining and may even see the benefit in getting to know other women in the church. Highlight new friendships when you can! Invite women to share how they've seen God's provision in placing them in their discussion group for Bible study or at a retreat.

When we moved to Kentucky, God placed three new residents – in a town with few transplants – in the same Bible Study Fellowship discussion group. We became the three musketeers, spending many days exploring our new town, experiencing new restaurants together, and uncovering treasures in nearby thrift stores. Adapting to our new community together helped to pull me out of the depression I had fallen into after our move. I have no doubt God orchestrated the arrangement so we could have a built-in support system to help each one of us adjust.

Model community. Encourage community. Talk about community. Lead a retreat or Bible study on community and hospitality. Share verses with your women that speak to community and unity on social media. Add community to your group prayers. You don't have to hammer the point home, but God can use the liberal sprinkling of community-minded words and thoughts to change the hearts of your women.

WELCOMING GUESTS

Due to extenuating circumstances and multiple moves, our family has had the opportunity to visit well over a dozen different churches. It's my least favorite part about moving. We try to narrow the field by investigating each church online first. Once we decide to attend, we do so with the intent of staying. With two boys in tow, a church has one chance to make a first impression. If things don't go well, we aren't likely to return.

After three Sundays of visiting "under the radar," we had completed and submitted the all-important visitor form. We checked the boxes of several ministries we were interested in knowing more about. Youth ministry. Check. Men's ministry. Check. Women's ministry. Check. We've jumped through these hoops at other churches, often receiving little or no follow up from ministry leaders. To be honest, we'd learned to keep our expectations low. Thank God this church was different! I have to admit I was pleasantly surprised to receive an email from the women's ministry director.

In her warm and welcoming email she:
- Let me know where I could find women's ministry news and info.

- Asked if I'd like to be included in the online women's ministry communication.
- Noted she was aware I had already signed up for the next Bible study session.
- Gracefully wove in the mission and purpose of their women's ministry.
- Included details and an invitation to the next women's ministry event.
- Invited me to contact her with any questions I had.

I felt welcomed! And in case you're wondering, at this point she had no idea that I have an online ministry for women's ministry leaders.

As Thom S. Rainer points out in *Becoming a Welcoming Church*, "Many church leaders and members think their churches are healthier than they really are. Many leaders and members think their churches have better ministries than they really do. And many leaders think their churches are friendlier than they really are."[19] This has sadly been our experience too.

There's a fine line to walk between making someone feel welcome and smothering them. Create and implement a plan for ensuring new faces are greeted warmly and introduced to others at every single women's ministry event – one on one, not a whole group introduction.

I've attended women's ministry events as the new girl and not had a single person approach me or welcome me. Unfortunately, I am not alone in this experience. Rainer explains, "Churches perceive they are a friendly church because the members are friendly to one another. But they don't think about walking in the shoes of first-time guests."[20] Your women probably are very friendly – to each other.

Include community building in your leadership training for all of your team members and volunteers. Don't assume women know how to be welcoming. Train them to make purposeful introductions and to engage women they see sitting on the sidelines. Help them to be aware of times they slip into holy huddles and cliques. Consider role-playing different situations so they can practice. Your team needs to model what they expect from those in attendance. If you don't want them to huddle and chat in the kitchen once women begin to arrive, then tell them in advance you expect them to circulate and talk to women they don't know well. Showing what you expect is powerful and eliminates questions and assumptions.

Quick Tips for Your Team

- Listen and ask questions. Sometimes we smother guests with talk about ourselves or the church. Get to know your guests. Identify *their* needs.
- Don't dismiss those who aren't new in town. They may not be as connected as you may assume.
- Warmly greet your women in the parking lot near the door you want them to enter. Many of them won't know which door they should enter.
- Utilize ushers to help guests find an empty chair if this might be a crowded event. It's super awkward to wander around looking for a space to sit.
- Before your event begins, share where the bathrooms are located and how best to get to them.
- Explain everything. If you're serving communion, explain how the elements will be distributed. If you want them to stand or sit down, tell them. If you're going to move to another room, explain how they'll get there and what they need to do when they arrive.
- Position greeters inside your event space, not just at the door. Train those greeters to look out for and connect women with others in a similar season of life or with similar aged children.
- Provide words for every song you sing. Use the screen, your programs, or both.
- Never assume prior knowledge of a biblical book, character, or concept. Always give background and context.

As a first-time guest it can be a challenge to figure out who is part of the event and who isn't. Purchase shirts for your team to wear, place stickers on name tags, use unique lanyards, or don an apparel item – such as a bandana or lei – that ties in with the event theme to help your team stand out in the crowd.

Do everything possible to make every woman feel welcome.

Is Your Team a Clique?

In some churches, the women's ministry team is a clique. Do your women see you as a tight-knit group that's hard to break into? Do you all travel together in a pack? Do you fail to include women outside of the team in your event planning or implementation? Are the faces women see on the stage or in the front of the room the same month after month and year after year? What can you do to change any perception that your team is a clique?

Every step we take to combat cliques by cultivating community is worth it.

Every step we take to combat cliques by cultivating community is worth it. Women long to belong. Women who feel included can't wait to return to the next Bible study or women's ministry event with a friend in tow.

○ ° ○ ° ○

Prayer

Lord help us to create a community for our women that draws them closer to one another and closer to You. Help us to warmly welcome guests. Please break apart any cliques that have formed among our women. Help us to love one another well. Amen.

PRAYER POINTS: WHAT IS GOD PROMPTING ME TO MAKE A MATTER OF PRAYER?

PP

_____

_____

_____

_____

_____

_____

_____

ACTION ITEMS: LIST THOSE THINGS UPON WHICH YOU SENSE GOD IS PROMPTING YOU TO TAKE ACTION.

AI

_____

_____

_____

_____

_____

_____

PART 2
Rethinking the Women's Ministry Framework

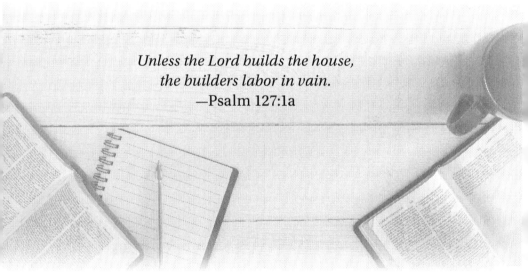

Unless the Lord builds the house,
the builders labor in vain.
—Psalm 127:1a

Chapter 4

Rethinking Teams

*Plans fail for lack of counsel, but with
many advisers they succeed.*
—Proverbs 15:22

WANT TO INVITE YOU TO RETHINK the structure of your women's
ministry team. If you're not currently using a team model, I'd like
you to pray about inviting others to do ministry with you. If your
team isn't functioning well, maybe God will highlight some changes
that would be beneficial. Let's remember the truth of Ephesians 4:16,
which states, "He makes the whole body fit together perfectly. As each
part does its own special work, it helps the other parts grow, so that
the whole body is healthy and growing and full of love" (NLT). That's
our goal – a healthy ministry that is growing and full of love!

*Lord, we ask You to reveal any way in which our women's ministry
team may not be healthy. Highlight any changes You want us to make
so we may grow and be full of love. In Jesus's name, Amen.*

ARE TEAMS NECESSARY?

Before we dive in, I have a confession to make; I am not a great team
player. Group projects make me cringe. I do not like to rely on others.
I'd much rather do it myself and know that it's going to be done right

and done well. God has been working on this issue of pride in me for many years. I'm learning to delegate and can see the benefits in the body of Christ working together. If you'd rather fly solo than sit on a team, know that I understand your struggle.

Romans 12:3–8 reminds us:

> For by the grace given to me I say to everyone among you not to think of himself more highly than he ought to think, but to think with sober judgment, each according to the measure of faith that God has assigned. For as in one body we have many members, and the members do not all have the same function, so we, though many, are one body in Christ, and individually members one of another. Having gifts that differ according to the grace given to us, let us use them: if prophecy, in proportion to our faith; if service, in our serving; the one who teaches, in his teaching; the one who exhorts, in his exhortation; the one who contributes, in generosity; the one who leads, with zeal; the one who does acts of mercy, with cheerfulness. (ESV)

1 Corinthians 12:17-26 continues this theme of team members with specific roles:

> If the whole body were an eye, where would be the sense of hearing? If the whole body were an ear, where would be the sense of smell? But as it is, God arranged the members in the body, each one of them, as he chose. If all were a single member, where would the body be? As it is, there are many parts, yet one body. The eye cannot say to the hand, "I have no need of you," nor again the head to the feet, "I have no need of you." On the contrary, the parts of the body that seem to be weaker are indispensable, and on those parts of the body that we think less honorable we bestow the greater honor, and our unpresentable parts are treated with greater modesty, which our more presentable parts do not require. But God has so composed the body, giving greater honor to the part that lacked it, that there may be no division in the body, but that the members may have the same care for one

RETHINKING TEAMS | **49**

another. If one member suffers, all suffer together; if one member is honored, all rejoice together. (ESV)

His Word makes it clear that when we use the different gifts God has given us, we create a united harmony that will point women to our Creator. We lay down our personal preferences for the benefit of the kingdom.

Practically speaking, when we ask women to serve in a specific role with specific responsibilities:

> *Team leaders who fail to define roles and responsibilities hinder the success of their team.*

- The hard work of hosting an event is shared among the members of the team.
- Team members refine and improve their tasks as they learn and adjust from one event to another, decreasing the chances that missteps or mistakes will be repeated.
- Unity among team members grows as they support the efforts of one another.
- Team members flourish as they serve in their area of gifting.
- Division of tasks is understood and respected.

Team leaders who fail to define roles and responsibilities hinder the success of their team.

How to Build a Team

Now that we've established that teams are good and necessary, let's work through how to build a team from the ground up. When God first called me into women's ministry, there was no team in place. The role of women's ministry director had sat vacant for about a year and a half. God had taught me a valuable lesson during the season when I led our Mothers of Preschoolers (MOPS) team that I'd need to apply to this new situation.

Before God called me into women's ministry, I helped to launch a new MOPS group in our church and served as the co-leader. We made many, many mistakes that first year, but one of our biggest mistakes was the process we used to fill our MOPS leadership team. We did not pray about the women we invited to serve. I know that critical misstep led to most of our troubles. It was a difficult and hard year with very little unity. God allowed us to reap the consequences of our disobedience.

That second year, though, God redeemed our MOPS group through a difficult breakup of our team and by way of a new MOPS mentor mom, Kim. Kim taught me how to prayerfully build a team. The difference between our two MOPS teams was startling! God led us to ask women that weren't even on my radar but were perfect for the task. There was a sweetness, a unity, and a spirit of prayer that permeated everything we did.

As the new women's ministry director, I replicated this process to build our new team. This two-step process will work whether you are recruiting new team members or adding to an established women's ministry team.

Step One –The List

Start by putting together a list of names. Pray that God will put women in your path. Expect Him to bring them to you. Keep your eyes open – they may not look like what you expect! Write those names down. Ask for suggestions from wise, godly men and women. Ask your pastors, pastor's wives, and trusted small group leaders for suggestions. Use suggestions from your women's ministry team, if you have one. As you ask for names, be specific. Explain what position you are looking to fill, what the role involves, and what kind of person you are looking for. For example: we are looking for someone warm, outgoing, and friendly to serve as our hospitality team leader.

Pray. You and your team need to spend time specifically in prayer over the person and the position. Ask the Holy Spirit to give each team member discernment. Ask God to confirm or remove the names on your list. If there isn't unity, set that name aside.

When your list is ready, submit the name(s) to the pastoral staff for approval. Your church may have certain requirements for women that will be serving in leadership roles. Church membership, active attendance, and personal recommendations are common prerequisites. Make sure you abide by those requirements.

Step Two – The Ask

When you've been given the green light to ask a woman to serve, please be intentional in your approach. You may wish to schedule a time to meet over coffee or call them on the phone. This is not the time to text or to grab someone in the hallway between services and pop the question! When we take the time to be intentional in the way in which we ask someone to serve, it communicates the need for prayerful consideration.

Introduce yourself and explain why you are calling. Let them know there is an opening on the women's ministry leadership team for [insert position] and their name was suggested. Side note: I never reveal my source, as it can add unwanted pressure to say yes, and that source may not share names with me ever again! If possible, share *why* they would be a good fit. For example, "Susie, you always make everyone feel welcome. God's given you a heart and a gift for hospitality."

> *When we take the time to be intentional in the way in which we ask someone to serve, it communicates the need for prayerful consideration.*

Ask them to pray about it, and ask them to call you back by a specific date. Kim, my MOPS mentor, suggested I give them one week to pray. My Bible Study Fellowship (BSF) teaching leader encouraged me to narrow that window down to just seventy-two hours. When I told her I would always give women a week, she challenged me – didn't I think God could give them an answer in three days?! I must admit waiting a whole week for a yes or no can drag out the process, especially if you receive multiple no answers.

Encourage them to seek scriptural confirmation. Many women don't know how to look and listen for direction from God through His Word. Encourage them to spend time in God's Word, asking God to give them a verse or passage that conveys a clear yes or clear no. I often share a recent personal example of how God did that for me.

If they are married, insist that they make certain their spouse is in agreement. You'll want their spouse to be supportive and understanding when ministry impacts family life and schedules.

Ask if they have any questions and answer them as honestly as you can. If they don't ask about what the position involves or team expectations (such as meeting monthly), share those with them. You don't have to get overly detailed at that point – just give them a general overview. You don't want to scare them off, but you also want them to understand the level of commitment that is expected.

End by praying for God's discernment for them. Yes, out loud, in person or over the phone with them.

Wrap it up. Thank them for their time and remind them that you look forward to hearing back from them by the date you've given them.

Tips:

- If they do not call you back on the designated day (and many of them will not), you need to call them the very next day. If they ask for an extension, give them one more day, no more. If God hasn't given them a clear yes by then, it's okay to assume His answer is no or not right now. If He wants them to be part of the team, He will do it some other way or some other time.

- Try not to take an answer, either yes or no, during that first phone call or contact. You want them to seek God's will and speak with their spouse. If they are adamantly against serving, end the conversation graciously and thank them for their time.

- If they say they are too busy, be understanding and sympathetic. If you can, kindly remind them that God can expand our time or may lead us to take something else off our plate to make room for something new. Encourage them to pray and seek God's will.

- Graciously accept the answer you receive. It can be really hard to get a no when you are confident God is calling them to serve. You've been obedient to ask.

I'll admit I used to dread these phone calls until God helped me to see what great opportunities they are. Even the no's have given me the chance to get to know some of our women better and have provided some great teaching moments about seeking God's will. They do get easier over time, and the benefits far outweigh my discomfort!

Please notice I did not suggest that you put a "help wanted" in your newsletter or church bulletin. You're recruiting women for a leadership position, and as such, there should be a vetting process. If you advertise an open leadership position, you limit yourself to those who apply, and if only one person responds, you're stuck with them. Author Sue Edwards issues this caution, "Don't be too quick to place women in positions of authority. Be sure they are the real deal, honest, teachable, and humble."[21] Just because someone is willing to serve doesn't mean they are called to serve.

> *Just because someone is willing to serve doesn't mean they are called to serve.*

WHAT ROLES DO YOU NEED TO FILL?

That very first women's ministry team began as a team of three, including me. That was it. For a church with about eight hundred members, that felt like a tiny team, but it was what God gave us, so we trusted Him. Slowly He added to our numbers. For retreat and conference planning, we created separate teams. It worked, even when it seemed it wouldn't. You don't have to have a big team for God to use you to encourage, love, and reach the women in your church and community.

My friend and former women's ministry leader, Gina Duke, recommends following the guideline of one team member for every one hundred women in your church. If you oversee a large women's ministry, you may want to max out at twelve with those leaders overseeing sub-teams. Make it a matter of prayer and trust God's timing and provision for your specific situation.

Prayerfully prioritize the team roles you sense God is leading you to fill. To start, you'll need a leader or co-leader, with duties divided, for your women's ministry team. Next, review your women's ministry mission statement and the church's mission statement. Let those statements guide the needs and roles of your women's ministry team. You'll also need to take into account which women's ministry needs are being met by other ministries in the church. Partner with them; don't replicate or compete with their efforts.

There are many different ways to structure your team. Consider roles that oversee ministry areas – Bible study and discipleship, missions, interest and support groups, and fellowship. Or you may wish to structure your team by tasks – childcare, decorations, event coordinator, food and hospitality, music and worship, new members and visitors, prayer, publicity, registration, retreats and conferences, secretary, and treasurer. Prioritize and pray. What works in one church might not work in yours. Give God license to create a team specifically for the needs of your women.

If you already have a team in place but no roles or responsibilities, decide as a team what roles are needed. Then consider having each woman take a spiritual gifts test. You may wish to meet one on one with each team member to pray about and discuss which role they feel would allow them to best serve using their gifts. If more than one woman feels called to a role, co-leaders may be the best option. It is possible that some of your women may step down during this process, in which case you can work through the process of adding new team members – this time with a specific role in mind.

A multigenerational team is more likely to birth a multigenerational ministry.

As you prayerfully recruit women to your teams, make certain your team includes women of different ages, stages, and different social circles. We need to hear from women who are different than us. If you find you're struggling to reach a specific age group, pray for a way to add them to your team. Many leaders struggle to reach younger women but have not asked a younger woman to serve on their team. Their insight and experience can help us to be more effective. A multigenerational team is more likely to birth a multigenerational ministry. Many leaders also find that including past team leaders and pastor's wives as advisors to the team is of great value. Their experience can provide invaluable insight and direction.

Rethinking women's ministry teams requires that we seek out the best person for the job. That may mean putting down our presumptions of what a women's ministry member should look like. I am so thankful that the leadership in my church didn't pass over me because I was a young mom with young children with zero experience leading a women's ministry.

Sometimes we assume the senior pastor's wife will take on the role of women's ministry leader. This form of nepotism can be problematic for the church. Not only may she not be the best woman for the job, she might not want the job! To my knowledge, no other ministry in the church operates in this way, nor should it. Our intent should be to prayerfully recruit women to whom God has given a gift and passion for women's ministry.

The process of building a team could take a few weeks, a couple of months, or it may be ongoing. God will not likely fill every role immediately. He may not ever fill them all! Get started and trust He'll add women to your team in His perfect timing.

How Long Should Women Serve?

Our sweet little team of three grew to seven before I was required to step down as the women's ministry director. Per our church by-laws, our women's ministry director was expected to serve a total of three years, with one year off before being able to serve again. Thankfully, our church did not have those restrictions for our women's ministry team members. If memory serves me right, we asked new women's ministry team members to make a two-year commitment.

If your church policy does not dictate term limits for your women's ministry leader or team members, this is something you'll want to discuss and create a policy on. There are pros and cons to term limits. I asked the leaders in my Facebook group to help me compile a list.

Benefits of term limits:

- Prevents leadership burnout.
- Protects the ministry from long-term damage if the leader isn't successful.
- Prevents personality-driven ministry.
- Provides the opportunity for other women to lead.
- New leaders can bring fresh energy and ideas to a stale ministry.

Possible negative impacts of term limits:

- There's a lack of continuity as each new leader casts a new and different vision.
- Some of the initiatives may not take root because every leader has her own thing she would like to do.
- Relationships that have been developed within the community during outreach projects may not continue with the new leader, as they may not find those outreach efforts of value.
- Great leaders are forced out of the role.
- The position may sit empty if a new leader cannot be found quickly, causing women's ministry events and activities to discontinue in the interim.
- We may be overstepping our bounds by removing someone who God has not called out of service.

Disadvantages of unlimited terms:

- Tired leaders remain in place to the detriment of the ministry.
- Women remain in roles where they may not be effective, gifted, or called.
- Leadership may be resistant to change, preferring to do things the same way they've always been done.
- Women may be unwilling to serve in a never-ending role.
- There may be no process in place for removing ineffective leaders.

Whether or not you or your church implements term limits, you'll need to create a process for knowledge transfer and training for new leaders. It's also imperative that church leadership reviews the effectiveness of women's ministry team leaders and has a process in place for replacing leaders when it is necessary.

We need to provide women a way to exit graciously when they sense God moving them into a different ministry.

We need to also provide women a way to exit graciously when they sense God moving them into a different minis- try. Many teams have found that asking leaders to recommit every one or two years helps to smooth that process. Staggering start terms can also increase the team's success by balancing the team with seasoned and new members.

Recommended Team Documents

Written job descriptions – Written descriptions help to clarify responsibilities and roles, which decreases the opportunities for team members to inadvertently step on each other's toes.

Team covenants – Team covenants can help ward off potential problems. If problems arise, covenants can serve as a reminder to the commitment team members have made. Think of them as an insurance policy – one you hope you never need. Consider including meeting attendance expectations, a confidentiality policy, conflict management guidelines, and communication standards. "Sample Job Descriptions" and "Women's Ministry Team Covenant" are included in the free bonus materials online.

THE NECESSITY OF VOLUNTEERS

Everywhere I've served, and even in the places where I haven't, I've seen this women's ministry mistake committed over and over again. And I'm not just throwing stones; I'm 100% guilty of committing it myself.

This one mistake:

- Increases burnout
- Dismisses the other women in the church
- Fuels pride
- Creates isolation

It's a mistake that is fixable. It's a mistake that is reversible. And it's a mistake you need to address and correct if your team is making it. Are you ready for it? **One of the biggest mistakes women's ministry teams make is not utilizing women outside of the women's ministry team.**

If you're thinking, oh, that's not us, hang with me for a couple more minutes. You may be surprised to find your team is guilty too! Think about your women's ministry team events.

Who brought the food?

Who sat at the welcome table?

Who served as prayer counselors?

Who decorated?

Who sat at the registration table?

Who served as Bible study facilitators?

Pull out a sheet of paper and write down the names if you need to. How many of those women are *not* on your women's ministry team?

Over and over, I've been a part of and witnessed teams that do it all themselves. Whether it's an issue of not wanting to bother other women (that's a lie, by the way), not making the time to make a few phone calls, texts, or emails, or hanging on to control, it's a problem.

When we exclude women of the church from serving at our women's ministry events, we:

- Create a clique
- Keep women from using their God-given gifts (1 Peter 4:10)
- Restrict other women from being a blessing
- Inadvertently hurt the feelings of some of our women
- Limit our reach

I get it. It's sometimes (okay, almost always) easier to do it yourself. It's a pain to communicate your expectations. It takes time to train others.

Here's the bigger problem – those excuses and reasons aren't biblical. God calls us to be part of a church body (Hebrews 10:24–25). God tells us to carry one another's burdens (Galatians 6:2). We are to work together in community with other believers (Ecclesiastes 4:9–12). The older women are to teach the younger (Titus 2:3–5).

When we ask women outside of our women's ministry team to bring food or serve, it does two big things:

When we involve as many women as we can, the women's ministry truly becomes the women's ministry.

1. **It allows other women to shine and serve!** Many women in your church would love to bring a snack to or serve at your next event. Bringing a dish or serving guarantees they will show up. And chances are they will bring a few girlfriends along with them. If you are struggling to get a specific generation to come to your events, ask them to bring some food or serve!

2. **It gives your team a break.** Seriously. Your team is already working hard to pull off the event. They don't need to be the ones making food and greeting women at the door for every single event. They are doing enough.

Tap some women who are welcoming to serve as hostesses. Call on some mighty prayer warriors to serve as prayer counselors. When it's time to add women to your team, you'll have a whole pool of women whose strengths you know and who have already dipped their toes into women's ministry. It's a whole lot easier to serve when you've already been made to feel as if you are part of the team.

When we involve as many women as we can, the women's ministry truly becomes the women's ministry.

Prayer

Lord, we want to assemble women's ministry teams that will bring You glory. Give us wisdom as we create our list of names. Prepare the hearts of those You are calling into service and give them a clear yes or no. Help us to build teams that reflect the needs of the women in our church. Please grant us discernment and excitement as we move forward. In Jesus's name, Amen.

PRAYER POINTS: WHAT IS GOD PROMPTING ME TO MAKE A MATTER OF PRAYER?

PP

_____
_____
_____
_____
_____
_____
_____

ACTION ITEMS: LIST THOSE THINGS UPON WHICH YOU SENSE GOD IS PROMPTING YOU TO TAKE ACTION.

AI

_____
_____
_____
_____
_____
_____
_____

Chapter 5

Rethinking Meetings

*Listen to advice and accept instruction, that
you may gain wisdom in the future.*
—Proverbs 19:20

NOW THAT YOU HAVE AT LEAST one team member, you'll need
to decide when, where, and how often to meet. In this chapter, we're going to delve into the logistics of women's ministry
meetings. We'll also take a look at who else you should be meeting
with regularly.

How often should your team meet? I've been on teams where we
met monthly, every other month, or as needed. My advice would be to
meet monthly. Going too long between meetings often meant we had
to pack a lot into each meeting. Meeting as needed left too much up in
the air. Would something come up that would require bumping our
next meeting up, or would we have to squeeze in two or three meetings in one month because we hadn't planned far enough in advance?
Who would decide when we needed to meet again?

Meeting monthly:

- Allows your team to touch base at regular intervals
- Provides an opportunity to address old and new business

- Offers consistency, especially when meeting on the same day, time, and place
- Keeps the team connected, especially beneficial in a larger church or one with multiple services
- Bathes your ministry regularly in prayer

Once you've determined how often you'll meet, you'll need to determine where you'll meet. We've had meetings at both the church and at team member's homes. While it's fun to meet at someone's home, driving distance could become a source of friction. Most team members likely live within easy driving distance to the church, making it a central meeting location. Meeting at the church also allows team members to grab supplies and provide onsite training when needed. Your church building is also a neutral meeting location. Some team members may feel they need to side with the hostess if meeting in her home, rather than offering their honest opinion. In either case, select a space that's comfortable, but also private.

When will we meet and for how long? I've been on teams that have met during the daytime and others that met at night. Daytime meetings can be convenient if your team members are available. However, I encourage you to be flexible and revisit your meeting time when new women join the women's ministry team. Only meeting in the daytime could keep women with inflexible work schedules or those who have childcare needs from being able to serve on the team. Likewise, if you have a team member that cannot drive at night, you'll need to arrange transportation so she can attend. As for your meeting length, I suggest scheduling monthly meetings for one and a half to two hours.

AGENDAS

Now that we covered the logistics, let's move onto the content. Every meeting should have an agenda. In most cases, your women's ministry team leader or co-leader will create the agenda, with input as needed from other team members. Having sat in meetings with and without agendas, I believe agendas directly impact the success of our meetings.

Agendas can:

- Give your team time to prepare and pray over agenda items by distributing your agenda before the meeting. No one likes to be surprised. Give God time to speak to their hearts.
- Ensure a level of accountability – both for you and for the team. If it's written down, it's more likely to happen.
- Keep the discussion on track and focused. I've often pointed to my agenda and reminded the team, "We have a lot to cover; we need to keep moving!"

Every meeting should have an agenda.

- When coupled with meeting minutes, agendas provide a reference for decisions and action items. Email a copy of the minutes to all team members no later than a week after you've met. You may also wish to keep a copy in your women's ministry binder to reference when a question comes up during your meeting.
- Model organization. When you are organized and prepared, it encourages and models that behavior for your team. While it may not come naturally to all of us, we can all learn to organize our meetings and thoughts.
- Remind team members of their responsibilities. If team members are expected to share an update, project, idea, etc., noting that on the agenda serves as a gentle reminder. I put the names of our team members behind agenda items for which they are responsible.

If at all possible, send out your meeting agenda one week before the team meeting. Use that email to remind your team of the meeting location and time. Be sure to attach to the agenda any other related notes, lists, and spreadsheets they will need. Sending out the agenda before the meeting allows women to make contact before the meeting if they have concerns or information to share. Those pre-meeting discussions can be extremely helpful to all of you! It also allows time for your team to gather and research any of your topics. The decorating team leader might want to search Pinterest for some ideas for an upcoming event. The publicity chair may want to mock up some flyers to bring and share with the group. And, as mentioned, the advance notice provides time to pray.

MEETING CONTENT

There is much you could, and much you should, cover when your team meets together. The women's ministry leader or co-leader should take charge and run your team meeting, moving along the conversation as needed and reining in the conversation if it gets off track.

You may wish to begin each meeting with an icebreaker game to build unity and develop relationships among team members. The better your women know each other, the better they'll be able to communicate with each other and extend grace to one another. Before you begin to plan out what God desires for your ministry, be sure to pray! Don't ask only for a blessing on your plans, but also ask God what He wants your team to do. Ask Him to direct and order your steps. Pray also for the women in your church and community. If your agenda is light, you may have time to pray for your women by name if you are in a small church. You may wish to follow that time with a short testimony, teaching from the Word, or a mini training. (See the worksheet titled "Women's Ministry Team Needs Assessment" in the free bonus materials online to help determine the training needs for your team.) Wrap up any old business left over from the previous meeting and then move into the upcoming events and activities. You can organize your agenda by event or by team member, or a combination of both.

Many leaders, including me, like to provide each team member with an opportunity to share praises and prayer requests with the

> *Don't ask only for a blessing on your plans, but also ask God what He wants your team to do.*

rest of the team. You may want to set a limit of two personal and two ministry-related requests.

If team members are working on an upcoming event or activity, a progress update should be expected. If you empower your team members, you won't need to use the bulk of your meeting time for event planning. Big decisions such as event themes, speakers, dates, and times can be set by either the women's ministry direc-

Your team members are busy women, and they appreciate efficient and effective meetings.

tor or by the event team leader. Smaller decisions such as napkin color and even program design should be delegated.

Francis Chan shares this great analogy in *Letters to the Church*, "Leaders have become like personal trainers who lift the weights for their clients. They run on the treadmill while their trainees sit and marvel," then wonder why people aren't developing.[22] If we want our leaders to grow, we have to give them opportunities to lead. You'll find your agenda moves along much quicker when leaders are able to report rather than debate decisions.

Creating a standard meeting agenda is another way to keep things running smoothly. Team members quickly learn what's expected. Your team members are busy women, and they appreciate efficient and effective meetings. Planning for meetings is also easier when there's a format in place.

SAMPLE WOMEN'S MINISTRY TEAM MEETING AGENDA

Icebreaker game or question
Group prayer
Teaching, testimony, or training
Old business
New business (listed out by topic or by position)
Action items (highlight who, what, and when)
Prayer

I find it helpful to decide in advance approximately how much time we'll need to discuss each item on the agenda. Though I only note the time for each item on my copy of the agenda, knowing that God may move us along a bit faster or slow us down for a needed discussion along the way.

PLANNING MEETINGS

Many women's ministry teams choose to have an annual all-day planning meeting to set the overall ministry plan for the year. Some teams even budget for a planning retreat. These meetings provide great opportunities for vision casting, leadership development, and team building. Include time for your team to reflect on what's working well and what changes they'd like to see.

Pastor Eric Geiger uses these three questions in the annual reviews of his team:

- What am I not doing that you would like me to start doing?
- What am I doing that you wish I would stop doing?
- What am I doing that is important to you that I keep doing?[23]

I'd suggest you tweak them a bit so the focus is on the ministry and planning ministry events (though asking the questions above can help assess the effectiveness of your leadership).

- What do you think God is asking our women's ministry to start doing that we are not doing?
- What do you sense God is bringing to an end or asking us to stop doing?
- What is our women's ministry doing that you feel God wants us to continue doing?

You could ask your team to work on these questions in small groups or in one large group. You could also provide these questions in advance of your planning meeting or retreat, allowing time for your team to process and pray over the questions.

MEETING WITH YOUR PASTOR

I used to dread meeting with the pastor that oversaw our women's ministry team. I was afraid of saying the wrong thing, not having the right answers, and presenting an idea and getting a big, fat no. Instead of meeting regularly, it was up to me to reach out when an issue came up, or I had to be summoned to the pastor's office if he had a concern. No wonder I was a nervous wreck! Had we met regularly, it would have significantly reduced my stress level, and our women's ministry would have benefited.

I had suspected that few women's ministry leaders meet regularly with their supervising pastor, so I included a few specific questions on a recent survey of 250 leaders to test my theory. Unfortunately, my suspicions were right. Of those surveyed, 28% said they rarely or never meet. But 33% said they did meet regularly (quarterly, every two to three months, or monthly). However, that also includes 17% of leaders surveyed who are the spouse of the pastor.

Many leaders commented that they meet as needed. Meeting when needed is a good thing, but there is also value in meeting consistently. This is not about micro-managing or a lack of trust as some leaders hinted. Women's ministry is a ministry of the church. Meeting regularly with our pastor ensures we are working together to further God's kingdom and encouraging the spiritual growth of our women. If the church staff or your pastor does not believe the women's ministry is supporting the church's mission, the future of women's ministry could be in trouble!

Meeting with your pastor regularly:

- Is biblical. Hebrews 13:17 makes it clear we are to submit to our leaders in the church. "Have confidence in your leaders and submit to their authority, because they keep watch over you as those who must give an account. Do this so that their work will be a joy, not a burden, for that would be of no benefit to you."
- Offers protection when conflict arises. Not only can your pastor provide wise, biblical counsel, but when accusations

are made or rumors fly, a good working relationship benefits everyone. If your pastor is already aware of the situation, they may be able to respond immediately. You want your pastor to be able to say with confidence when a problem comes across their desk, "That doesn't sound like Patricia. Let me talk with her, and then I'll get right back to you."

- Allows you to share specific prayer requests and praises. Share what God is doing through the women's ministry. Offer a few stats and stories. Your pastor can't pray specifically for the women's ministry if they don't have the details. We all need as much prayer coverage as we can get! Ask your pastor to share your requests with the rest of the church staff when applicable.

Meeting with your whole team may overwhelm your pastor and may not be the best use of their time or your team's time. Instead, women's ministry team leaders or co-leaders should meet with the pastor and report back to the team.

Even if your pastor trusts you and your team to minister to women without regular meetings, I want to encourage you to schedule short thirty-minute meetings quarterly. You may need to make an official request to meet with your pastor. Explain why you'd like to meet with them and use some of the benefits listed above. Hopefully, they won't need to be convinced that meeting regularly benefits everyone.

If you are an unpaid volunteer, like the majority of leaders surveyed, there may be no precedent for meeting with your supervising pastor. Ask the Lord to help you word your meeting request. Start by requesting just one meeting and go from there.

Quick tips for meeting with your pastor:

- Keep it brief. Make notes about what you want to discuss.
- Consider providing questions in advance so they can be prepared to answer them.
- Keep your emotions in check.
- Share more stats and facts than stories.
- Be gracious and grateful.
- Accept the answer and process it later.

- Thank them for their time.

If your pastor is unwilling to meet, pray over the situation and send brief status updates quarterly. God may change their heart and mind in time.

MEETINGS WITH VOLUNTEERS

Women are more likely to volunteer if you provide training for the task. If you are asking women to serve as prayer counselors or discussion group leaders, please meet with them at least once before your event. Taking the extra time to prepare your volunteers will pay off! Written instructions on their own are not enough. Review them with your women, as some will not have read them or read them thoroughly. Be sure to address any questions in advance to minimize hiccups at the event. Don't forget to verbalize your appreciation for their time and dedication. Be certain to pray over and for them before you send them on their way. Volunteers that feel prepared are going to serve with greater confidence. When we view volunteers as a blessing and not a burden, other women see the beauty of the body working together in unity.

Surveys can provide some great feedback, but even more powerful is a conversation with your target audience.

FOCUS GROUP MEETINGS

Surveys can provide some great feedback, but even more powerful is a conversation with your target audience. Many leaders find gathering specific groups of women together to be incredibly helpful. For example, if your ministry struggles to reach young moms, invite a handful of young moms to meet with one or two women from your team. Ask them how the women's ministry can support them. Ask what they would like to see you offer and what needs they have that you could meet. Ask open-ended questions, listen, and write down what they say. Take that information back to your team for discussion.

You may wish to gather several women – some from each genera-tion – for coffee once a year to chat informally about women's ministry. You'll not only get much more detail than you would on a survey, but you'll be able to ask follow-up questions to understand any issues or concerns that are shared. Pre-select questions to guide your time together. Examples: What women's ministry event would you like to see repeated? What activity or event encouraged you to take action? Which event challenged you to grow spiritually?

Again, listen and record their responses. Limit your comments to follow-up questions and resist the temptation to defend decisions that were made.

ARE YOU LISTENING?

Some of the most disturbing comments on the women's ministry survey I conducted came from women who felt their leaders and lead-ership team were not open to new ideas.

> *"It is a select tight-knit group of a few who do all plan-ning ... they plan around their own needs and wants without welcoming any new ideas."*

> *"There are also control issues; new ideas have been shot down without consideration."*

> *"Leadership is typically about who is queen bee and who that queen bee likes."*

> *"I've offered ideas, only to be shot down or not supported."*

> *"Women in leadership are afraid of new women who would like to enter in with ideas and suggestions."*

> *"The women in our church have repeatedly asked for more times of fellowship and sharing; however, the leadership seems to think there is no room for that."*

You can hear the hurt in these responses. We can do great damage to our ministry and the relationships with women in our church when we fail to consider the advice and ideas they offer. Rarely is an imme-diate answer required. It's worth the time it takes to circle back with a response that has been prayerfully considered through the lens of the ministry's purpose and mission. Even "no" answers provide an opportunity to strengthen relationships. May the Holy Spirit give us words to respond in love.

Navigating Difficult Personalities

The topic never seemed to matter; if Sasha (not her real name) was present at our meeting, I could almost always count on her to dis-agree. I felt as if every idea I offered was placed under a microscope and examined thoroughly. I tried not to let her get to me, but there were meetings when I had to fight back tears. Though I knew she was just as passionate about women's ministry as I am, we rarely saw eye to eye.

Perhaps you've had to deal with a "Sasha" on your team or an equally difficult personality. You may have even begged God to let you quit. As Sue Edwards and Kelley Matthews point out in *Leading Women Who Wound*, "Personal attacks, difficult people, and conflict are all inevitable in ministry." [24] If we prepare ourselves and our team to handle conflict biblically, we all benefit. The Bible tells us how we are to handle disagreements.

> If your brother or sister sins, go and point out their fault, just between the two of you. If they listen to you, you have won them over. But if they will not listen, take one or two others along, so that "every matter may be established by the testi-mony of two or three witnesses." If they still refuse to listen, tell it to the church; and if they refuse to listen even to the church, treat them as you would a pagan or a tax collector. (Matthew 18:15-17)

Sadly, we rarely see this method of conflict management exer-cised in the church. In your team covenant, you may wish to instruct team members to follow Matthew 18:15-17 when navigating conflict and disagreements. Edwards and Matthews remind us, "A wise leader understands that Satan *loves* to use conflict to destroy ministry."[25] Be proactive, not reactive.

I have found that praying together and developing relationships among team members can help lessen the potential for conflict. Grace is extended more readily when women have background information about each other. Include time for team building in your agenda.

This chapter was packed with food for thought! I hope you've marked several sections with a PP (Prayer Point) and AI (Action Item). If we want to improve ourselves and our ministries, we have to be willing to make some changes.

Prayer

Lord, please bless our meeting with others. May we use our meeting time wisely. Help us to be receptive to feedback that can improve our leadership and reach more women. Guide us as we navigate any disagreements or conflict. Keep our focus on You and Your will for our ministry. Amen.

PRAYER POINTS: WHAT IS GOD PROMPTING ME TO MAKE A MATTER OF PRAYER?

PP

ACTION ITEMS: LIST THOSE THINGS UPON WHICH YOU SENSE GOD IS PROMPTING YOU TO TAKE ACTION.

AI

Chapter 6

Rethinking Bible Studies

Give me understanding, so that I may keep your
law and obey it with all my heart.
—Psalm 119:34 (NIV)

BIBLE STUDIES ARE OFTEN THE BACKBONE of a women's ministry – and with good reason! God is clear in His Word that we are to understand, obey, and preserve His law (see Psalm 119:34). A strong, healthy Bible study program is often the sign of a healthy women's ministry.

Before you write off this chapter as one you don't need to read, let's take a quick health assessment of your Bible study program. As you respond, consider all of the women in your church, not just those you see and interact with regularly.

How healthy is your Bible study program?

1. Does your Bible study schedule meet the needs of all of the women in your church?

☐ All ☐ Most ☐ Some ☐ None

2. Do you offer childcare for your Bible studies?

☐ All ☐ Most ☐ Some ☐ None

3. Do your women regularly read and study the Bible on their own?

☐ All   ☐ Most   ☐ Some   ☐ None

4. Do your women understand and apply basic biblical truths?

☐ All   ☐ Most   ☐ Some   ☐ None

5. Do your women have an overall understanding of the Bible from start to finish?

☐ All   ☐ Most   ☐ Some   ☐ None

6. Does your discussion time challenge and encourage your women to grow spiritually?

☐ Yes   ☐ No   ☐ Probably not; it's rather short

7. Do you provide training for your Bible study group facilitators and teachers?

☐ Yes   ☐ No   ☐ Not sure

8. Do your Bible study groups meet together regularly outside of their scheduled class time?

☐ All   ☐ Most   ☐ Some   ☐ None

How did you do? Did God highlight a few areas that might need a bit of rethinking and refinement? Or maybe you weren't quite sure how to answer. I'll be honest; I assumed our women's personal Bible study habits were pretty decent until we administered the Bible study habits survey. ("Bible Study Habits" is included in the free bonus materials online.) My heart sank as I flipped through the cards they had filled out anonymously. Did our women *really* feel they have a preschool or elementary understanding of God's Word? Do they *really* find God's Word boring? Outside of Sunday mornings, our women were not spending much time in God's Word at all. I suspected that was true but didn't want it to be. It was clear to our team that this was an area on which we needed to focus.

I pray, as you walk through the following areas of Bible study that may necessitate a tune-up, that God will be clear in pointing out which things you need to mark with as a PP (Prayer Point) or an AI (Action Item).

CREATING A BIBLE STUDY SCHEDULE
THAT WORKS FOR ALL WOMEN

Initially targeting stay-at-home moms, many Bible study programs focus primarily, or solely, on daytime Bible study offerings. However, as we acknowledge that our target audience has changed, we need to find ways to offer studies that meet the needs of working women, single women, and single moms, most of whom are unable to attend the typical daytime Bible study. We need to expand our perspective and our Bible study schedules.

For over a year, our women's ministry team prayed for God to clear the path so we could begin to offer an evening study. Armed with a survey from our women that showed the need and desire for an evening study, we approached our senior pastor. He was quick to agree that this was a need but asked that we hold off for now. He did not want to take away from the attendance of the current Wednesday night church program or create a situation where women had to choose.

We need to find ways to offer studies that meet the needs of women who are unable to attend the typical daytime Bible study.

As we waited and prayed, we began to see God prepare the way for a women-only evening Bible study. In addition to mixed discussion groups at the Wednesday night church program, the staff started to offer a women-only discussion group option, which was well received. Months later, the church staff decided to move away from Wednesday night programming, which opened the door for the team to offer women's evening Bible studies at the church. The response was immediate and significant! A church with an average Sunday worship service of about 175 managed to draw thirty women to the evening Bible study, in addition to those twenty-five to thirty who attended the morning Bible study sessions.

We need to make certain our Bible study schedule provides a variety of times and opportunities for women to attend. Take a survey to discover what days and times your women are available. While it's unlikely you'll be able to meet every single need, you'll see some clear patterns of days and times that work for most. The church we currently attend offers five different women's Bible study options. One is very early in the morning before most start their workday. Another is at night. Think outside the box!

MEETING THE NEED FOR CHILDCARE

I know how very hard it is to try to find reliable childcare workers. I've been tasked with creating the schedule, recruiting the workers, and dealing with last-minute worker cancellations. The hard truth is that when we fail to provide childcare, we prohibit a large group of women from attending. Not everyone can afford a babysitter or has a husband who's home and willing to watch the kids in the evening. Limiting childcare to preschool age and younger also leaves out homeschool moms.

As you seek to meet your needs for childcare workers, first go to your children's pastor or director. Find out what the guidelines are in your church for adult-to-child ratios at each age level and what type of training is required. Background checks should be required for everyone who works with children. Ask if they have a list of workers they can share with you – many do! Other sources for childcare workers include preschool substitute lists, homeschooled teenagers (daytime), other teenagers (evening studies), retired women, MOPS childcare workers, women with school-aged children who aren't working full time outside of the home, and volunteers from within your Bible study.

It's best if you can find, or even pay, someone to coordinate childcare for your events and Bible studies. It is a massive undertaking between finding workers and providing Bible-focused content for those in their care. Please pay your workers, unless they insist on serving. Paychecks encourage commitment. Gift cards or small gifts at the end of each study are also appreciated. You may have to build childcare expenses into your budget or charge a small fee. Don't forget to ask for donations if church policy allows. Most women, even if they don't need childcare, understand and appreciate the necessity.

THE REALITY OF BIBLICAL ILLITERACY IN OUR CHURCHES

We are facing a Bible literacy crisis in the church. Christians proclaim to believe the Bible, but they aren't spending much time reading the Bible. According to The Barna Group, practicing Christian millennials say "Bible reading is more important than other spiritual disciplines."[26] However, when asked, only 30% actually practiced the discipline of reading the Bible in the last month. Unfortunately, this trend is not limited to millennials. Women who have been attending Bible studies for years struggle to read and study the Bible on their own.

In the summer of 2016, as we wrapped up another Bible study book session, the Lord began to convict me of the time I had spent in the Bible study book versus the time I had spent reading His Word. There was a big discrepancy. I was humbled and embarrassed at how little time I had spent in my Bible while in "Bible study." All summer long, I wrestled with the Lord over what needed to change. I didn't have a seminary degree, so how was I supposed to study the Bible

Women who have been attending Bible studies for years struggle to read and study the Bible on their own.

on my own without a book, pastor, or author guiding me? I devoured Jen Wilkin's *Women of the Word: How to Study the Bible with Both Our Hearts and Our Minds* [27] and Francis Chan's *Multiply: Disciples Making Disciples*.[28] Researching different Bible study methods, it was clear the tried-and-true AIO method (application, interpretation, and observation) worked and needed to be the foundation of what I sensed God calling me to do.

By the end of the summer, the READ Bible study method was born, and I presented the rough draft to our Bible study coordinator over lunch. I walked her through the steps – Record, Explore, Apply, and Do – and shared with her the rough drafts of weekly worksheets that would lead women through the Bible, dig deep into one chapter a week, and serve as the basis for our group discussion time. Denise shared that the team had been praying for almost two years for God's clear direction for an inductive type of Bible study class. She agreed to review the materials and adopt the READ format for the next year. Our women dug deep into four books of the Bible and learned how to uncover the cultural and historical context of the text. We watched God transform our women through the regular reading and studying of His Word!

I cannot emphasize enough the importance of biblical literacy. Social media feeds are filled with Scripture that has been taken out of context and quotes that are biblically inaccurate. Jen Wilkin warns, "Both the false teacher and the secular humanist rely on biblical ignorance for their messages to take root, and the modern church has proven fertile ground for those messages. Because we do not know our Bibles, we crumble at the most basic challenges to our worldview."[29] Our women need to know what the Bible says and how to discern the accuracy of a Bible study book, a Christian celebrity's message, and even their pastor's sermon.

WOMEN WANT MORE TIME TO DISCUSS GOD'S WORD

The READ Bible study technique answered an unspoken need in our Bible study groups: women were hungry for more discussion time. This wasn't a unique need. Women in Bible studies everywhere are worn out from lengthy Bible study videos and short discussion sessions. As one woman commented on the women's ministry survey I conducted, "There is little conversation, little chance to pour into each other. Just the video lady."

As we rethink and restructure our Bible study schedules, we need to include time for our women to engage with the lesson.

Discussion groups allow women to:

- Process what they've studied
- Practice talking about God and the Bible

- Learn from other women (Titus 2:3-5)
- Hold one another accountable

As the beta group for the READ Bible study method, we surveyed our women several times to ensure they were growing and engaging in their groups. With almost forty women registered, we had divided our women into three smaller discussion groups, each with a facilitator whose role was to lead them through the worksheet questions and keep the group on topic. Our discussion group time ran for almost an hour, and it was by far our women's favorite part. Here's just a sample of what they had to say:

As we rethink and restructure our Bible study schedules, we need to include time for our women to engage with the lesson.

> "We had a wonderful discussion group; everyone participated and many new thoughts on different Scriptures [were] revealed."

> "I loved our group! I loved the various ages and stages in life. The Bible speaks so much about the wisdom of age, and I truly benefitted from the ladies and their experience."

I never failed to be amazed at how God would use that discussion time to teach us more about Himself and to encourage one another.

SELECTING THE BEST BIBLE STUDY FOR YOUR WOMEN

I'm willing to wager that your regular Bible study girls have a favorite Bible study author. And while that isn't a bad thing, many of our women have become dependent on someone, often a specific someone, to lead them through the Bible. It's time we stop unintentionally fueling the belief that our women are not capable of studying the Word without a well-known author at the helm. I can't help but wonder what Jesus thinks of all of this. I wonder if He sits there sighing, shaking His head, and musing, "Girls, I gave you the Holy Spirit and the Bible. You have all you need."

A well-known Bible study author should not be a requirement for selecting a Bible study. As I've already mentioned, your women can and should learn how to study God's Word on their own. I also realize that there are many fabulous Bible studies women would label as "life-changing." So how do we decide what to do?

We must blanket our Bible study selection with prayer and listen for the Lord to direct us to the next best study for our specific group of women. We also need to determine *who* will make the Bible study selection for our groups. The group facilitator, a pastor, a women's ministry team Bible study coordinator, a Bible study review team, attendee vote, or a combination might select your study. Here's a quick look at the pros and cons of each one.

Facilitator Selection

Pros – The facilitator is likely to pick a study topic she is passionate about, and that passion will shine through in her teaching and facilitating.

Cons – Facilitators sometimes get in a rut, repeatedly choosing the same authors. The selection(s) may not be in alignment with the current focus for the women's ministry or the church.

Pastor Selection

Pros – The women's ministry team does not have to delegate the task. The pastor is often aware of newer studies. The studies they choose will likely align with the current church focus or mission.

Cons – If the pastor is a man, he may not choose something that appeals to a large number of women. The facilitator and women's ministry team may feel they had no say in the selection.

Women's Ministry Team Bible Study Coordinator Selection

Pros – This is her primary role so she should be familiar with a variety of studies and should have her pulse on the interests of the women in the church and community. As part of the women's ministry team, her selections should support and encourage the current focus of the women's ministry and the church.

Cons – Her preferences for a specific study style or author may be weighed more heavily in the decision-making process, though not necessarily intentionally. A facilitator may wish to have input.

Bible Study Review Team Selection

Pros – A wide variety of women come together to review and give input. A member of the women's ministry team or the Bible study coordinator should chair and guide the team, keeping them on task and in alignment with the current church and ministry goals. Multiple people complete reviews of the same study.

Cons – There is a time commitment, and multiple meetings will be necessary. The majority tends to rule, which may not always be a good thing.

Attendees Vote on the Selection

Pros – Those who attend are given a voice in the choice(s). If the women's ministry team or Bible study coordinator is struggling to narrow down the options, this can be a fair way of deciding which study or studies to offer.

Cons – The voters may be unfamiliar with the content of each study. The final selection may not be in alignment with church and ministry goals. Not all votes may be bathed in prayer.

One option with this is to have attendees vote on the topic, but not on the specific study materials, which allows the facilitator to make sure the study is one that aligns with God's Word and the church's beliefs.

☙

As each group prayerfully reviews the studies in light of Scripture, there are some key questions you'll want to answer.

First, the practical questions:

- Who will be participating in this study?
- What is the biblical literacy level of the women who will be attending?
- Is this a topic, book, or character of the Bible that is of interest to the group?
- How long is your meeting time?

- How many weeks will you be meeting?
- How much homework do you wish to assign?
- Do you need/want specific questions for your discussion time?
- What is your budget?
- What type of study are you looking for? (Bible, DVD-driven, Bible study book, Bible study workbook, combination, or sermon-based)

While there's some wiggle room in the answers to the practical questions, the theological questions are deal breakers.

Theological questions:

- Is this study biblically sound?
- Does this study emphasize engagement with the Scriptures, or it is focused primarily on the author's personal stories and experiences?
- Does the study encourage women to read and apply the Word of God to their lives?
- Does this study align with the beliefs and teachings of my pastor and church?
- Does the study encourage prayerfully seeking both understanding and knowledge through the teaching of the Holy Spirit?
- Does this study encourage women to search the Scriptures for answers, or are they primarily found within the pages of a book or workbook?

As Jen Wilkin states in *Women of the Word,* "Sound Bible study transforms the heart by training the mind, and it places God at the center of the story. But sound Bible study does more than that – it leaves the student with a better understanding of the Bible than she had when she started. Stated another way, sound Bible study increases Bible literacy."[30]

How we select our Bible studies matters. When we base our Bible study selections off of a popularity vote, we very well may miss selecting the best study for our women.

RAISING THE BAR

I can no longer remember the source, but I have not forgotten the lesson presented in my education class at The University of North Carolina–Chapel Hill. When we set the bar high, our students will rise to meet it, but when we set the bar low, our students won't work to rise above it. The same holds true for Bible study. I've heard leaders say:

"Our women won't do homework."

"They only like studies with a DVD."

"We don't want to scare new or young Christians away."

I hear the concern and love behind these excuses, but that is exactly what they are – excuses. We assume we know what's best for our women, often to the neglect of their spiritual growth.

Years ago, a dear friend of mine, Melissa, decided she wanted to join Jen and me for the Beth Moore Bible study at our church. Melissa had never attended a Bible study before, and we were pretty sure she hadn't made a personal decision to follow Christ yet. Jen and I were tempted to discourage Melissa from coming. We assumed she might find it a bit (okay, a lot) overwhelming, and we knew the homework would be extremely challenging. To this day, I thank God that Melissa came. That first week, we discovered she needed a study Bible in a translation that was going to be easier for her to read. We purchased a new Bible and placed tabs in it to help ease some of her frustration in flipping from book to book.

Encourage and expect your women to complete each week's homework.

Isaiah 55:11 reminds us, "So is my word that goes out from my mouth: It will not return to me empty, but will accomplish what I desire and achieve the purpose for which I sent it." Melissa heard God's Word during our time together. She may not have grasped every concept, but she grew, and she experienced the beauty of women studying God's Word together. I am so glad we didn't tell her she shouldn't come.

Encourage and expect your women to complete each week's home-work. Set the bar high, but also extend grace when they fall short. Our women should never be made to feel less than because they didn't complete the homework for the week. Trust that God's Word will not return empty and that what they hear and what they do study will transform their hearts and souls. If we only offer milk, our women will never move on to the meat of Scripture (see Hebrews 5:12–14).

BIBLE STUDY FACILITATORS AND TEACHERS NEED SOLID, REGULAR TRAINING

While we lived in Kentucky, I was called into leadership as a small group leader for Bible Study Fellowship (BSF), an international, non-denominational community Bible study. Each week we attended a leaders' meeting where we reviewed the week's lesson in preparation for leading our group discussions the next day and where we received intentional training. Some weeks we participated in role-playing exercises. Other weeks we worked through how to handle specific needs and situations. There was a level of accountability, community, and intentionality like none I had ever experienced. That experience forever changed my view of training and had a profound impact on how I led my group and related to my group members.

Many Bible study coordinators rely upon and rotate through the same Bible study teachers. Their list of solid, reliable Bible study teachers is short, but they aren't quite sure how to expand that list. Creating a process for recruiting and training new leaders is critical. I find many women say no because they don't have the skills, but they are willing to learn if given the opportunity. If you're not sure if your church offers training, ask! Sometimes, unintentionally, small group leaders receive training, but women's Bible study leaders have been forgotten.

Many churches are seeing the need to train up leaders and have begun offering in-house group leader training. Some churches have purchased online training programs and require all new leaders to complete the program. You can also create apprentice-style training for your leaders and require them to shadow and receive mentoring from another leader. Some churches require new Bible study leaders to co-lead for one study with a seasoned leader; others place women's ministry team members in the Bible study class for support and encouragement. Put a process in place to train your leaders, and you'll see your leaders and your groups flourish!

ENCOURAGE COMMUNITY BEYOND THE SCHEDULED BIBLE STUDY CLASS TIME

Julie's invitation to grab lunch after our first Bible study meeting meant more to me than she'll ever know. We had moved from North Carolina to Kentucky in early July when the heat kept everyone indoors or sent them splashing in the pool. I'd met few people and was aching to connect with some other moms. Her invitation was a lifeline to my depressed soul. I was desperate for community!

Over the years, I've had the opportunity to be a part of Bible studies that encouraged community and others that did not. I've witnessed the change in dynamics, and greater depth of sharing that can happen when women build relationships beyond the one to two hours they are in Bible study together.

In one church, the leaders scheduled regular, optional lunches every other week. Group members were emailed in advance with the date and location, with every effort made to select restaurants that were child friendly and affordable. At Bible Study Fellowship, childcare arrangements were made so that about four times per year we could meet thirty minutes early for a light breakfast and fellowship. In alternating months we'd gather at a group member's home after Bible study for fellowship and bagged lunches. Our host would provide drinks and dessert. Holiday parties and service projects are also great ways to build community among your Bible study girls.

We also encourage community when we leave the door open for women to join our Bible study groups after the initial start date. Women aren't going to wait around for your Bible studies to open up again; they are going to go elsewhere. We know God can use even one week in the Bible study group to whet a woman's appetite to sign up for the next study. Let's say yes when women ask if there are any openings in Bible study.

As Bible study leaders, we can build relationships and community by connecting one on one with group members in between meetings. In addition to weekly email reminders to the whole group (homework reminder, word of encouragement, weekly announcements), I recommend that leaders take the time to connect with at least a third of their group members each week via a personal phone call, text, email, or a handwritten note. Reach out to women who were absent and let them know they were missed. Follow up with the answer to a question that was asked. Thank Felicia for sharing what God revealed

We can build relationships and community by connecting one on one with group members in between meetings.

to her through the lesson that week. Pray with Camden as she seeks to minister to her ailing mother. Our group members will see Christ through us as we show love to them and minister to them.

ONLINE BIBLE STUDIES

IRL (in real life) neighborhood and church Bible studies are facing some tough competition from online Bible study offerings. I suspect this debate about the digital church is just beginning. As I mentioned at the beginning of the book, many of your younger women may not differentiate between online and IRL relationships and gatherings. They've found connection and fulfillment in both kinds of relationships. Most of your older women, however, may strongly favor IRL relationships over those online. While we cannot yet quantify the impact of online versus IRL Bible study, there are some significant differences worth pointing out.

Online Bible studies offer benefits that cannot be ignored, including convenience, flexibility, and the potential to interact with people around the world. In today's overscheduled world, Bible study in pajamas at any time of the day can be a real draw for many women. Working women may not have a Bible study option at their church that fits their schedule. Chronic illness, lack of childcare, and caring for elderly parents can all hamper participation in local Bible studies. On the flip side, online studies offer little accountability. Women who aren't participating can easily fall through the cracks. Online Bible study leaders are unlikely to follow up or remain connected with each woman once the study ends.

IRL Bible studies offer a different kind of community experience. Leaders can encourage members of the church to minister to one another during their group time and in the days between. Leaders who fall under the authority of the local church will support the church's mission and beliefs. IRL groups provide opportunities to practice hospitality at church and outside fellowships. Leaders and members can follow up with one another and continue connecting long after the Bible study ends. Even if video tools are used, sitting face to face, IRL leaders can read and address nonverbal cues that would otherwise remain hidden. Our goal should always be to encourage our women to meet together as was modeled by the early church. As your team prayerfully examines what is best for your women, take a look at Acts 2:42, Colossians 3:16, Hebrews 10:24–25, 2 Timothy 4:3, Matthew 28:19–20, and Titus 2: 1–8.

Prayer

Lord, I pray that studying the Word with other women would be life changing for the women in our church. Develop a hunger and desire in them for Your Holy Word. As we study Your Word together, bond us together, and deepen our relationships with one another and with You. Lord, as Psalm 119:18 says, open our eyes that we may see wonderful things in Your law. Amen.

PRAYER POINTS: WHAT IS GOD PROMPTING ME TO MAKE A MATTER OF PRAYER?

PP

_____

_____

_____

_____

_____

_____

ACTION ITEMS: LIST THOSE THINGS UPON WHICH YOU SENSE GOD IS PROMPTING YOU TO TAKE ACTION.

AI

_____

_____

_____

_____

_____

_____

Chapter 7

Rethinking Testimonies and Devotionals

But how can they call on him to save them unless they believe in him? And how can they believe in him if they have never heard about him? And how can they hear about him unless someone tells them?
—Romans 10:14 NLT

SAT THERE, STUNNED. HAD GOD BROUGHT this woman to share her testimony solely for my benefit? Our speaker's story was almost identical to my story. She had put into words something I had been struggling to articulate. Much like me, she recounted her years growing up in church, attending church functions, but being completely unaware there was more to God than Bible stories and Sunday school lessons. It wasn't until her early adult years that someone helped her to understand that God wanted to know her personally. He desired a relationship with her. Hearing this woman's testimony deeply affected me. I had placed my testimony in the pile of "too boring to share." Somewhere along the way, I had developed the belief that all testimonies required drama, dire circumstances, and intense emotions. Not true.

Perhaps you, the women on your team, or the women in your church also have become acclimated to high-stakes testimonies worthy of the big screen. In this chapter, I want to challenge you to rethink your approach to testimonies and devotionals. Let's set aside our previous experiences and assumptions and examine how every-day stories can impact our women for eternity.

What Is a Testimony?

A testimony is often defined as the personal retelling of the moment of conversion. It's a story of an encounter with Christ, the moment of salvation. The Merriam-Webster Online Dictionary defines a religious testimony as "a public profession of religious experience." While a testimony is and can be about the singular point at which we accepted Christ, a testimony can also communicate any experience we've had with Christ.

Why Do We Share Our Testimonies?

Despite the powerful testimonies you've no doubt heard or read, we don't share testimonies to elicit an emotional response. Those of us with less dramatic stories aren't off the hook. God makes it clear in His Word that all believers have a responsibility to tell others about Him.

> Give praise to the LORD, proclaim his name; make known among the nations what he has done. (1 Chronicles 16:8)

> But how can they call on him to save them unless they believe in him? And how can they believe in him if they have never heard about him? And how can they hear about him unless someone tells them? (Romans 10:14 NLT)

> Always be prepared to give an answer to everyone who asks you to give the reason for the hope that you have. (1 Peter 3:15)

> Be wise in the way you act toward outsiders; make the most of every opportunity. Let your conversation be always full of grace, seasoned with salt, so that you may know how to answer everyone. (Colossians 4:5–6)

But you will receive power when the Holy Spirit comes on you; and you will be my witnesses in Jerusalem, and in all Judea and Samaria, and to the ends of the earth. (Acts 1:8)

But you are a chosen people, a royal priesthood, a holy nation, God's special possession, that you may declare the praises of him who called you out of darkness into his wonderful light. (1 Peter 2:9)

Praise be to the God and Father of our Lord Jesus Christ, the Father of compassion and the God of all comfort, who comforts us in all our troubles, so that we can comfort those in any trouble with the comfort we ourselves receive from God. (2 Corinthians 1:3–4)

Did you catch the commands in these Scriptures? We are to make His name known, we need to be ready and able to answer when someone asks why we have hope, and we must not miss the opportunity to share with unbelievers. We are called to be God's witnesses, and we are to declare the praises of the One who called us out of the darkness and into the light. We are to comfort others as we have been comforted.

We share testimonies:

- To help our women view life with an eternal perspective
- To encourage one another
- To give hope
- To create connection
- To model obedience
- To inspire our women to look for God's fingerprints in their current situations and circumstances
- To provide testimony of God's faithfulness and love
- To open the door for sharing the gospel

There are times in which our women may not be able to feel God or see God clearly, but hearing others reflect on God's faithfulness in difficult circumstances can be an encouragement.

HOW DO WE SHARE TESTIMONIES?

As Donald S. Whitney so plainly states, "We should all be able to talk about what the Lord has done for us and what He means to us."[31] While on the surface that statement rings true, applying it is a whole other story! Even if the idea of sharing your testimony doesn't freak you out, it likely terrifies most of the women you know. A slight tweaking or rethinking of our approach may be all that is needed.

Let's talk about sharing our stories, instead of our testimonies. That simple word swap can remove a lot of pressure. Stories are familiar; they are comforting. We read them to children before tucking them into bed. All stories have a beginning, middle, and an end. Our stories should be presented similarly.

However, rather than modeling our stories after a children's book, God's provided us with numerous examples in the Bible of people who encountered Him, and their lives were changed. Joshua, Mary, Paul, Jacob, Noah, the woman at the well, Job, Ruth, and the list goes on. Let's take a quick look at one such story in the book of John. John 9 tells the story of Jesus giving sight to a blind man. When asked what had happened, the blind man replied, "The man they call Jesus made some mud and put it on my eyes. He told me to go to Siloam and wash. So I went and washed, and then I could see" (v. 11). While our testimony might not be as short as those three sentences, the format is one we can apply to our stories as we share them.

Swapping the word "stories" for "testimonies" can remove a lot of pressure.

1. The story consists of three parts: how I was, what happened, and how I am now.
2. The story focuses on what Jesus did.
3. Transformation is celebrated.

So how do we get started writing out our story?

1. Ask God to highlight something recent He has done in your life. If you journal, it may be helpful to thumb through recent entries.
2. Prayerfully jot down some notes about what you think God wants you to share. Highlight how I was, what happened, and how I am now.
3. Share a Bible verse that God used in that situation, circumstance, or season to refine, free, or encourage you. Celebrate the transformation.
4. End on a note of encouragement. We all have struggles that God uses to help us to be more Christlike.

Remember the three Cs:

Current – Focus on a recent lesson. Within the last year, if possible. Keeping it current reminds women that God is always at work!

Concise – Remember that this is not a speaking or teaching session. What you share should last between five and ten minutes, no more! Practice sharing it. Record yourself and listen to make sure your story is coming across as intended. Make a few notes so you don't lose focus.

Christ centered – Keep it focused on what God has done, not on dramatic details. It's about Him, not about you. You want your women to remember what God accomplished through you or the circumstance. When our eyes are focused on God, others see that and can learn by our example.

You'll find "Share Your God Story" included in the free bonus materials online to help you record and share the details of your story.

A few words of caution:

- Please, please, please do not share anything that would embarrass someone or lead to gossip.
- Protect your spouse, your family, and anyone who is a part of your story.
- When sharing with a group, you want to be more general than specific.
- Be prayerful and careful with details you share.

- You almost always need to get permission and input from any-one that is a part of your story. For example, if you are sharing about a hard season in your marriage, your spouse needs to be completely aware and on board with what you are sharing.
- Use caution when asking women to share about their current issues or struggles. We want to remove any chance that their story be driven by any anger or bitterness. Ask God for dis-cernment as you review their written story. It may be better for them to share when they have journeyed a bit further or healed a bit more.

May our stories be a reflection of 2 Corinthians 1:3–5, "Praise be to the God and Father of our Lord Jesus Christ, the Father of compassion and the God of all comfort, who comforts us in all our troubles, so that we can comfort those in any trouble with the comfort we ourselves receive from God. For just as we share abundantly in the sufferings of Christ, so also our comfort abounds through Christ."

As Nancy DeMoss Wolgemuth says, "Teach out of what God showed you when you messed up and didn't trust Him – where you ended up, where God found you. Teach from the addictions you've battled, the choices you should have made, the pain you could have avoided. Open the Word, open your heart, share the hard questions you've wrestled with, and watch God create beauty from ashes right before your eyes."[32]

FINDING WOMEN TO SHARE THEIR STORIES

Now that you have the tools to craft your own story and coach other women through sharing theirs, we need to identify who God wants to have share.

- **Pray before you ask.** Ask the Lord to lead you to a woman who has a specific story to share. Look for women who have found peace and healing and can clearly see God's hand in the situation.
- **Make a specific ask.** Ask her to share about a specific event in her life. Ask her to pray about sharing her story.

- **Have her write down the story that she'll share**. Recording her story will help her to process and plan which parts and pieces should be included and which should not. Give her a copy of the "Sharing Your Story" worksheet found in the free bonus materials online.
- **Read her story.** Check to be sure the story focuses on God's role and the transformation or change that occurred. Help her weed out any unnecessary or distracting details.

If you've exhausted your list of women to ask, speak to one of your pastors or small group leaders. They'll likely have some solid recommendations for you.

WHAT ARE DEVOTIONALS?

Devotionals are written testimonies, usually written by an author or Christian speaker. Did you catch that? Devotionals are *someone else's story.* Women's ministry meetings often include a devotion read out of a book, copied from the internet, or maybe even shared via video.

I understand the temptation to read the words written by someone else. When I first started as a women's ministry leader, I had a file of other people's stories to share at our meetings. If a book had an interesting short story, I'd turn down the corner of the page and read it to our women. I printed out heart-warming stories from the internet on more than one occasion. I know it's easier to share other people's stories than our own. Like grabbing a fast-food meal in a drive-through, sharing a devotional we've found online or in a book is convenient and feeds our women, but it isn't what's best.

When our women hear other women share what God has done in their lives, it makes a greater impact than any devotional read out of a book.

When our women hear other women in the church share what God has done in their lives, it makes a greater impact than any devotional read out of a book ever could. Suddenly it's personal. It's someone we know. And your women begin to believe that maybe, just maybe, God can help them too. Rather than recycling a devotional story from a book or the internet, let's build connections, share personal stories (aka testimonies), point women to Christ, and offer hope.

TEACHINGS ARE NOT DEVOTIONALS

The word devotionals is also used interchangeably with messages or short teachings. Once again, we're muddying the water of both our purpose and women's expectations. Most of your women equate the word "devotional" with devotional books (that contain stories from Christian authors often centered around a Scripture verse). All too often, devotions are light, short stories that are focused on making the reader feel good. Devotionals signal we're staying in the shallow end and we don't think our women can handle something deep.

What if, instead, we just said, "Sherry is going to share a short message from God's Word"? Make it clear to your women that the focus isn't going to be on man's words, but God's words. A great teacher will use stories to help communicate the message of God's Word while keeping the focus on the Word of God.

DO WE HAVE TO SHARE THE GOSPEL?

"Preach the gospel at all times; use words if necessary" is often falsely attributed to St. Francis of Assisi and sometimes even mistaken for Scripture. Despite its popularity, this sentiment cannot be found in God's Word. God tells us we are to use words, not just actions: "How can they believe in him if they have never heard about him? And how can they hear about him unless someone tells them?" (Romans 10:14 NLT).

That isn't to say that our actions don't speak loudly and draw people to Christ. As author Donald S. Whitney explains, "Often it is the message of the cross *lived and demonstrated* that God uses to open a heart to the gospel, but it is the message of the cross *proclaimed* (by word or page) through which the power of God saves those who believe its content. No matter how well we live the gospel (and we must live it well, else we hinder its reception), sooner or later we must communicate the *content* of the gospel before a person can become a disciple of Jesus."[33]

That first difficult year of MOPS, which I mentioned previously, our team went to great lengths to model "lifestyle evangelism" as we lived the gospel without words. It was our hope and prayer that our actions would point the moms in attendance to Christ. We intentionally omitted the gospel from all but two of our MOPS meetings. As an outreach-focused ministry, we did not want to offend non-Christians in attendance. We were devoted to love them like Jesus and love them to Jesus.

Certain that our actions were enough, we watered down our prayers so they weren't "too preachy" and our meetings were almost always practical and rarely religious. It was as if we put God in a box and told Him to stay there and not come out until we had properly prepared our women for His presence. *What were we thinking?!*

I remember talking to my sister-in-law, a pastor's wife, about the situation. She challenged me to consider who we were pointing our women to. If the focus was on our actions, were we pointing our women to Christ or ourselves? As I mulled over her words, I began to see the error of our ways. We had failed to point our women to Christ. Withholding God's Words robbed our women of the truth. We could not save them; only Jesus, through His sacrifice on the cross, could save them.

Is then, a regular, verbal sharing of the gospel message what's best? Our family has attended churches that have issued a weekly altar call where all who desired could come forward to pray to accept Christ as Savior. We've also attended a church with a strong focus on reaching non-believers that focused on the *why* but rarely on the *how*. Your church likely has a process and procedures for sharing the gospel. Your team may not feel that every women's ministry event or activity warrants a verbal presentation of the gospel. However, I encourage you to include the *how* – either verbally, written, or via invitation. Provide a tract or brochure that provides the steps for accepting Christ as Savior or invite women to speak to a prayer counselor or women's ministry team member. If God truly is everything we claim He is, women want and expect an introduction!

For more years than I care to admit I was not prepared to share the gospel. You may need to provide training so your leaders can share the gospel with confidence. Perhaps you'll want to take ten minutes at each of your meetings in the next year to share one of the many ways they can share the gospel. You'll find a list of gospel sharing tools in the resource list at the back of this book.

If God truly is everything we claim He is, women want and expect an introduction!

Crafting personal testimonies and sharing the gospel can be intimidating to our teams and our women, but they don't have to be. Trainings for your team and workshops with your women can equip them to share their testimony and the gospel. As Nancy DeMoss Wolgemuth says, "Whenever you've seen God prove Himself faithful, wherever His Word has sustained you in weakness and provided needed direction, and yes, even wherever you have experienced the consequences of *failing* to walk according to His Word – there's your story to share."[34] With a bit of intention, prayer, and preparation, sharing our stories and sharing the gospel can become regular, anticipated experiences at your women's ministry meetings and events.

O ° O ° O

Prayer

Lord, in the same way as 2 Corinthians 2:14 says, help us to spread out "the aroma of the knowledge" of You everywhere through the sharing of stories. Help us to train our team in communicating the gospel. May we make the most of every opportunity You give us to point women to Christ. Amen.

PRAYER POINTS: WHAT IS GOD PROMPTING ME TO MAKE A MATTER OF PRAYER?

PP

_____

_____

_____

_____

_____

_____

_____

ACTION ITEMS: LIST THOSE THINGS UPON WHICH YOU SENSE GOD IS PROMPTING YOU TO TAKE ACTION.

AI

_____

_____

_____

_____

_____

_____

_____

Chapter 8

Rethinking Mentoring and Discipleship

One generation commends your works to
another; they tell of your mighty acts.
—Psalm 145:4

THE BIBLE IS RIPE WITH EXAMPLES of mentoring and discipling relationships, including Ruth and Naomi, Mary and Elizabeth, Moses and Joshua, and Eli and Samuel. It isn't a matter of *should* we disciple or mentor, but *how* do we disciple or mentor. Traditionally, women's ministries have focused on mentoring, both organic and intentional. In recent years, discipleship has edged out mentoring as the trendy, updated approach. As many churches embrace large-scale, church-wide discipleship programs, women's ministry leaders are left wondering what their role is.

In this chapter, we'll uncover the differences between mentoring and discipleship. We'll examine the barriers that keep women from discipling or mentoring others. We'll work through solutions to those barriers as we seek to determine God's best plan for our women. Remember to keep a pen handy to mark your PP (prayer points) and AI (action items)!

WHAT'S THE DIFFERENCE?

Do you remember learning that a square can be a rectangle, but a rectangle can't be a square? (It was a concept I struggled to grasp!) Well, mentoring and discipleship have a similar relationship. Though you'll find some people use the two terms interchangeably, discipleship can be mentoring, but mentoring is not always discipleship. The differences may seem subtle, but as we prayerfully consider discipleship or mentoring as an arm of our women's ministry, we need to be intentional with our words. We need to decide which tool – discipleship or mentoring – will help us to reach our goal.

It isn't a matter of should we disciple or mentor, but how do we disciple or mentor.

Feeling confused? Until I did a little wrestling and some research, I was too. So many books have been written about discipleship and mentoring; I thought it best to look to the experts for our definitions.

Kandi Gallaty, in her book, *Disciple Her: Using the Word, Work, & Wonder of God to Invest in Women*, defines discipleship as "intentionally equipping believers with the Word of God through accountable relationships empowered by the Holy Spirit in order to replicate faithful followers of Christ."[35]

Janet Thompson, author of *Mentoring for All Seasons: Sharing Life Experiences and God's Faithfulness*, believes mentoring should be: "more than a typical friendship, include discipling when appropriate, always focus on spiritual maturity," and "address the numerous mentoring needs during the multitude of seasons in a woman's life."[36]

You'll notice both definitions include intentionality and relationships. Their aim and approach, however, are different. Discipleship utilizes the Word of God to equip believers and replicate faithful followers of Christ. Mentoring addresses needs, discipling when appropriate, to bring about spiritual maturity. The end goal is similar – spiritual maturity – but the approach is different. There is also an additional focus with discipleship on replication. One could argue that the Bible tells us we are to do both – disciple and mentor others.

To add some clarity to our discussion, I crafted a chart that highlights the possible differences and similarities between mentoring and discipleship. You may find your church or your own experience is more of a blend of the two.

	Mentoring	Discipleship
Time frame	May or may not have a specific end date	Has a definitive start and end date, often 12–18 months
Curriculum	Sometimes uses a program or book as a guide, but not always	Uses God's Word; might use a guided workbook or journal
Focus	Relationship and encouragement; spiritual growth through everyday life	Spiritual growth through the study of God's Word
Participants	Usually the pairing of a spiritually older woman with a spiritually younger woman	Most often occurs in small groups of six or fewer, can occur one on one, has a trained group leader
Approach	Usually organic	Organized, rarely organic
Frequency	May meet regularly, but might not	Meets regularly, usually weekly
Style	May be structured, but most likely not	Structured meetings, regular assignments
Goal	Guidance through a specific season, growing maturity, or teaching a skill	Growth and replication (disciples become leaders of discipleship groups)

Before we dive deeper, you may be wondering if discipleship groups are the same as a Bible study, Sunday school class, or small group. I'd argue, in most cases, no. Most of the latter often have a greater fellowship focus and less of an academic purpose.

Bible studies, Sunday school, and small groups frequently use Bible study books, not books of the Bible. These groups are often mixed-gender, larger classes, while discipleship groups (or D-groups as some call them) are same-gender, smaller groups of two to six. These smaller discipleship groups often benefit from increased accountability and a greater level of participation. So we don't get distracted or confused further, we're going to keep our focus on mentoring and discipleship.

The Bible supports both mentoring and discipleship. Titus 2:3 is probably the verse most often referenced by fans of mentoring, "Likewise, teach the older women to be reverent in the way they live, not to be slanderers or addicted to much wine, but to teach what is good."

Fans of discipleship love Matthew 28:19-20, "Therefore go and make disciples of all nations, baptizing them in the name of the Father and of the Son and of the Holy Spirit, and teaching them to obey everything I have commanded you. And surely I am with you always, to the very end of the age."

Psalm 145:4 is another verse that points to the importance of passing along our faith, "One generation commends your works to another; they tell of your mighty acts." And then there is this Psalm:

> My people, hear my teaching; listen to the words of my mouth. I will open my mouth with a parable; I will utter hidden things, things from of old – things we have heard and known, things our ancestors have told us. We will not hide them from their descendants; we will tell the next generation the praiseworthy deeds of the Lord his power, and the wonders he has done. He decreed statutes for Jacob and established the law in Israel, which he commanded our ancestors to teach their children, so the next generation would know them, even the children yet

to be born, and they in turn would tell their children. Then they would put their trust in God and would not forget his deeds but would keep his commands. They would not be like their ancestors – a stubborn and rebellious generation, whose hearts were not loyal to God, whose spirits were not faithful to him. (Psalm 78)

The command is clear, but how do we discern which approach is best for our women? We need to prayerfully determine our goal. Is our goal to form relationships that focus on encouraging spiritual growth through everyday life? Or is our goal the regular reading of God's Word together in a small group over a period of time, to develop disciples that will disciple others? Do we want an intentional, structured program or an organic program?

Organic Versus Intentional

Within mentoring and discipleship, there are two different approaches, organic (informal) or intentional (formal). Organic mentoring and organic discipleship form most often out of an established relationship. A younger woman may ask an older woman if they could study a book of the Bible together, or could she offer biblical advice about a specific situation. Often the relationship occurs without a verbal ask or a label. While they may decide to meet regularly, meetings are more fluid as they are often "doing life together" and meeting as needed. Organic mentoring rarely uses a program or set of materials. No two organic mentoring or discipleship relationships will look the same.

Intentional mentoring and discipleship almost always utilize a format or a program. Women may fill out profiles and receive their mentoring match via email or at a mentoring launch event. Mentors and mentees in the program may follow a set schedule, utilize a reading plan, or complete a workbook together. On the other hand, discipleship groups may be formed via personal invitation or registration similar to a Bible study signup. Discipleship groups (D-groups) read the Bible together, sometimes focusing on a chapter each day or each week. D-groups usually record answers or reflections in a journal or workbook, which are discussed during their weekly meeting time. Intentional mentoring and discipleship have a definitive start and end to their time, such as six, twelve, or eighteen months. Additionally, mentors and discipleship leaders often receive formal training and support.

For many years, I was a big proponent of organic mentoring, in part because I was on the giving and receiving end of organic mentoring. Kim, our MOPS mentor mom, mentored me informally for many years. Lois, one of my prayer partners and friends, also served as an informal mentor. We even tried to launch an organic mentoring program at one church without success. Organic mentoring is challenging to implement as a ministry initiative. Like a flower without regular watering, ministry initiatives without regular guidance and encouragement don't often flourish. Rather than pursue organic mentoring as a ministry initiative, trust that God will bring about deeper relationships over time. Organic mentoring should occur naturally among your women as they develop relationships with one another. Intentional mentoring and discipleship ministry initiatives are more likely to provide the structure and accountability that many women need.

Intentional mentoring and discipleship ministry initiatives are more likely to provide the structure and accountability that many women need.

BARRIERS TO MENTORING AND DISCIPLESHIP

Mentoring and discipleship programs can be intimidating! Often women feel they aren't godly enough, spiritual enough, prayerful enough, or fill-in-the-blank enough to be a mentor or discipleship group leader. The time commitment required can be a deterrent. With overloaded schedules, the idea of meeting weekly (or even regularly) with another woman is not realistic or appealing.

As leaders, we can remind our women they have wisdom to share and that God doesn't require perfection. We're all still "under construction," but the lessons they've learned along the way can benefit the women behind them.

Three Key Trainings That Will Empower Your Women to Mentor or Disciple

1. Teach your women how to read and study the Bible. This is something every woman can learn, and it is imperative that women are comfortable and confident to do so if they are expected to encourage the spiritual growth of those God has put in their care.

2. Teach them how to pray out loud. Most of your women are not comfortable praying out loud. It can be awkward, and we worry too much about what other people will think. Provide opportunities for them to practice. Share tools such as the ACTS prayer method that will give them the confidence to pray out loud.

3. Teach them how to tell their story. As we just discussed in chapter 7, our women need to be able to share what God has done and is doing in their lives.

Providing training in these areas will prime the pump for a mentoring or discipleship program launch. (See the section at the back of the book for a list of books and online resources.)

Despite our efforts and encouragement, not all of our women will accept an invitation to be a part of a mentoring or a discipleship program. That's okay. As your women mature spiritually, God will give them a desire to be in intentional, Spirit-driven community with one another. Pray fervently that God will draw those He desires to participate. We need to be faithful to invite women to participate, but their attendance is not in our control.

Rather than stress about the size of our groups or program, let's focus our energy and time on preparing and equipping our women so they can step with confidence into the role of mentor or discipleship leader when God calls them.

HOW TO LAUNCH A MENTORING OR DISCIPLESHIP PROGRAM

Chances are, discipleship or mentoring won't top the list of desired activities on your women's ministry survey. If God is leading you to launch a discipleship or mentoring program, you're going to need to:

1. Introduce your women to the concept.
2. Answer the question, "What's in it for me?" (WIIFM)
3. Train your leaders.

While it may seem unbiblical to market a ministry initiative, most of your women need a bit of encouragement, and many need full-out convincing! Provide the information in a winsome way and let the Holy Spirit do the calling and convicting.

Many years ago, our women's ministry team in Kentucky felt the Lord leading us to launch a mentoring program. We spent months praying. We formed a mentoring planning team that reviewed almost a dozen mentoring books and programs. We weighed the pros and cons of each, seeking what God wanted for our women. Once our selection was made, we planned a mentoring interest meeting.

Before that interest meeting, we introduced our women to the concept of mentoring at our annual women's ministry banquet. After our worship team sang the song, "Side by Side," we invited three church members – Kristyn, Jeannie, and Bettie – to share their personal experiences with mentoring. Kristyn, the youngest, was being mentored by Jeannie, and Jeannie was being mentored by Bettie, our senior saint. It was a beautiful picture of how we should be pouring into the lives of those coming up behind us and always seeking out wisdom from those ahead of us. Our theme for the year was "One Another," and God orchestrated it all together as only He could. Before our women left that evening, we announced the date and time of our mentoring interest meeting.

There are many other ways you can introduce mentoring or discipleship to your women. Workshops, kick-offs, book clubs, and Bible study books can all be used to gently introduce women to the idea of learning and growing together. Testimonies can be an extremely powerful and persuasive way to convince women that it really does work, and it can be fun!

In addition to taking the time to properly launch your mentoring or discipleship initiative, create a process and procedure for recruiting mentors and discipleship group leaders. As we discussed in chapter 4, just as members are recruited to the women's ministry team, these leadership positions should be approached with great intention and prayer. Invest time in training your leaders. Roleplay; work through different scenarios and complete a lesson together. Help them get comfortable with the task ahead. If you're using a program or curriculum, make sure they have ample lead time to review it.

Don't be discouraged by a small start! Seek to be obedient to God's leading and trust Him to grow the program in His perfect timing.

Don't be discouraged by a small start! Seek to be obedient to God's leading and trust Him to grow the program in His perfect timing.

Assessing Your Program

If God leads you to implement a mentoring or discipleship program, it is necessary to continually assess its effectiveness. Are things working? Do we need to make some tweaks? Do we see spiritual growth? How will we measure spiritual growth? Don't allow measuring spiritual growth to be a stumbling block.

I want to recommend a resource for measuring spiritual growth. Pastor Robby Gallaty lays out five characteristics of a disciple in his book, *MARCS of a Disciple: A Biblical Guide for Gauging Spiritual Growth*. Gallaty evaluates the effectiveness of discipleship groups in light of Matthew 28:19-20. These **MARCS** ask the question, are members **M**issional, **A**ccountable, **R**eproducible, **C**ommunal, and **S**criptural?[37] While spiritual growth is more difficult to assess than event attendance, with work, it is possible and necessary.

In addition, I encourage you to survey participants. Find out what their experience has been. You may want to assess their spiritual growth as well as the format of the program.

Sample survey questions:

- How would you rate your spiritual growth in the last six months?
- How would you rate your prayer life?
- How would you rate your confidence level in studying God's Word?
- How would you rate your sensitivity to the Holy Spirit?
- How would you rate your obedience to the Word of God?
- Describe any change in attitude toward studying your Bible.
- Have other people noticed Christ at work in you? If so, how?
- What were your group leader or mentor's strengths?
- What would you recommend be done differently the next time?
- How did you benefit from the homework?

Review the feedback and prayerfully make any needed adjustments.

WHAT IF YOUR CHURCH ALREADY HAS A DISCIPLESHIP OR MENTORING PROGRAM?

If God has led your team in this direction, you'll need to schedule a meeting with those ministry leaders. Share with them that God has burdened your team for greater discipleship or mentoring for your women. Ask the ministry leaders how you can partner with them to get more women involved. You want to complement, not compete with their ministry efforts. Can you host an event that focuses on discipleship or mentoring? Can you invite the ministry leader to a women's ministry meeting to share the signup process? Can you provide support to those women who are mentoring or leading discipleship groups? Be prayerful and respectful. Your offer may not be well received, or it may be embraced. It may not be God's timing yet. Plant seeds and water them with prayer.

If our church is already focused on mentoring or discipleship groups, any program we put into place should support the church and not pull women out of D-groups or mentoring relationships.

FINAL THOUGHTS

As author Janet Thompson points out, "We would never think of sending our babies out on their own as soon as they could walk and talk. Yet we send baby Christians out the doors of our churches into the secular world without a hand to hold to keep them safe until they become spiritually mature."[38] This is not just a task for the church; we have a role as women's ministry leaders to prepare and support our women. We can provide a biblical map and trained tour guide to help them navigate through this life.

Whether or not mentoring or discipleship is the tool, we have a scriptural responsibility to make disciples who make disciples.

Whether or not mentoring or discipleship is the tool, we have a scriptural responsibility to make disciples who make disciples. Nancy DeMoss Wolgemuth offers this challenge to older women, "We have to ask ourselves: *Have we fulfilled our responsibility as an older woman?* Have we modeled the beauty of an ordered life, lived under the control and lordship of Christ? Have we been faithful in reaching out to our younger sisters, teaching what is good, and training them to live a life that honors Him?"[39]

○　∘　○　∘　○

Prayer

Lord Jesus, forgive us for any time that we've failed our responsibility to teach and encourage our sisters in Christ. Give us the wisdom to know what discipleship or mentoring needs to look like in our ministry. Help us to find ways to encourage biblical sisterhood through our events and offerings. Amen.

PRAYER POINTS: WHAT IS GOD PROMPTING ME TO MAKE A MATTER OF PRAYER?

PP

_____

_____

_____

_____

_____

_____

ACTION ITEMS: LIST THOSE THINGS UPON WHICH YOU SENSE GOD IS PROMPTING YOU TO TAKE ACTION.

AI

_____

_____

_____

_____

_____

_____

Chapter 9

Rethinking Service Opportunities and Missions Projects

*Do not merely listen to the word, and so
deceive yourselves. Do what it says.*
— James 1:22

YOU MIGHT BE ONE OF MANY women's ministry leaders who is tempted to skip over this chapter assuming this one doesn't apply to your ministry. Someone else in your church may oversee service, outreach, and missions. Your church may even separate women's ministry from women's missions. As we continue this journey of rethinking, I want to ask you to prayerfully consider how the practice of separating or delegating missions to another group in your church may not be what's best for your women or your ministry.

WE'RE ALL CALLED TO SERVE

Something incredibly beautiful happens when women answer God's call to serve. Relationships deepen and shared experiences provide unbreakable points of connection. We move from sisters in Christ who sit side by side at an event to being the hands of Jesus, serving side by side in the community. We move from being a part of the church to *being* the church.

Service opportunities and missions projects often appeal to women who may not attend the typical women's ministry events or fellowships. Millennial and author of *The Passion Generation: The Seemingly Reckless, Definitely Disruptive, But Far From Hopeless Millennials*, Grant Skeldon, knows that if your church struggles to reach and involve millennials, getting them to serve outside of the church inspires them to serve inside the church.[40] We broaden our reach and obey God's Word when service and missions become a part of women's ministry.

NURTURING MISSIONS-MINDED WOMEN

Would you describe your women as missions minded? Do they have a burning desire to share the gospel with those who are lost? Do they want to serve others? Do they seek out opportunities to love those in need in your community? Do you see your women actively loving their neighbors?

While only God can transform sinful hearts into servant's hearts, there is much we can do to nurture that transformation. We can provide regular opportunities for our women

While only God can transform sinful hearts into servant's hearts, there is much we can do to nurture that transformation.

to serve others. Varying those types of offerings allows your women to participate in missions on different levels, some of which they may find comfortable, and others that may stretch and grow them.

Four levels of missions participation:

1. **Prayer** – This is probably the easiest and first step for many. As women pray for missionaries, mission trips, outreach projects, and for the lost, their hearts begin to soften toward others in need.
2. **Donations** – Donations of money or goods can be a launching point for future work with a ministry. When your team becomes aware of a need, it's easy to add a request for

donations to the next women's ministry event. Examples include food drives for a local food pantry, diaper drives for a pregnancy center, and bottled water for hurricane victims.

3. **One-time service projects** – One-and-done projects allow women to see the beginning and end of a project and may stoke interest in forming an ongoing relationship with the beneficiaries. Assembling back-to-school gifts for teachers is one example.

4. **Relationships** – When we enter into community with others, we can build godly relationships that extend far beyond prayers, donations, and one-time service projects. Partnering long term with a local parachurch ministry can be fruitful for those serving and those being served. Over time, your women may have opportunities to share the gospel and form discipling relationships.

We want to give our women multiple and different types of opportunities to serve others, encouraging them toward community and relationship. However, before we prayerfully seek out a new ministry partner or project, we need to have a clear understanding of what ministries and missions projects our church is already committed to and involved in. Remember, we want to complement, not compete.

Building Relationships with Parachurch Ministries

Where can your women join in where God is already at work? There are likely several parachurch ministries in your community that need regular volunteers. Again, start by checking with those your church already has a relationship with.

Several years ago, our women's ministry team helped to coordinate a food, cleaning supplies, and toiletries drive for a local women's shelter that our church partnered with. Little did we know how dropping off those supplies would change the direction of our women's ministry! Let me give you a little background first, so you can understand how God had already planted the seeds for this partnership.

A few months before the food drive, our women's ministry team had rewritten our women's ministry statement. This was our new mission statement:

> To glorify God through prayerfully planned activities and events for women in our church and community, which promote spiritual growth and lead women to Christ. We seek to serve women, both locally and internationally, with love and grace.

Through that process, God led us to a rather startling discovery; we weren't actively serving women locally or internationally. Like many other women's ministry teams, we were doing a great job of feeding the women in our church, but we neglected to look beyond our church walls and into the community. The answer wasn't to take an eraser to this new mission statement, but to prayerfully seek ways to serve.

We began to pray and asked God to show us what He would have us add to our women's ministry calendar. When we dropped off the donations, one of the women on our team casually asked the director if there were any other needs we could help with. A meeting followed, and the next thing I knew we were bringing in lunch and participating in an afternoon of pampering with the women at the shelter.

That was only the beginning of what God was going to do! We made no-sew fleece blankets for them with plans to make more *with* them. We brainstormed ideas for game nights and craft nights. God didn't just light a fire for missions in our team members, but other women in the church wanted to be a part of ministering to these women too! God surprised us all when the director at the shelter provided transportation so the women could come to the church for events. Several women even attended our trunk-or-treat event with their kids!

We never knew how long these precious ones would be at the women's shelter, but that did not matter. We embraced the opportunity God had given us to show them His love for however long we had a connection. God moved in the hearts of our women in a mighty way.

God can do the same in your community! I pray He'll direct your steps and help you to develop healthy relationships within your community.

WHO ARE THE PEOPLE IN YOUR NEIGHBORHOOD?

If asked, I could only tell you the names of maybe ten people on our street of more than forty homes. After nearly five years of living in this neighborhood, I'm sad to say I haven't made more connections, despite Jesus's command in Matthew 22:37-39 to love my neighbor. As Amy Lively plainly states in *How to Love Your Neighbor Without Being Weird*, "It's pretty hard to love someone when you don't even know their name."[41]

God has placed your women in neighborhoods filled with people who need Him and don't know Him. Perhaps God wants your women's ministry to equip and encourage your women to become local missionaries, serving and loving the people on their street. May we embrace the call to serve and love in Galatians 5:13–14, "You, my brothers and sisters, were called to be free. But do not use your freedom to indulge the flesh; rather, serve one another humbly in love. For the entire law is fulfilled in keeping this one command: 'Love your neighbor as yourself.'"

What about the communities in your church neighborhood? Is there a school nearby, an apartment complex, a trailer park, or a fire station where God is prompting you to build relationships? Rather than invite the women in the nearby apartment complex to come to the church for Bible study, what if you took Bible study to the apartment complex every week?

Before you make excuses, pray, and ask God to show you solutions. It's probably going to be messy and inconvenient, but most worthwhile ministry is!

Are there women who are already coming to the church building regularly but are not staying? Preschool moms. Basketball moms. Moms dropping their children off for Vacation Bible School (VBS). Moms bringing a van-full of middle schoolers to youth group. Invite those women to stay, rather than drop and run. Pray about whether

God wants you to provide coffee and conversation or something more structured. One church leader recently reached out to me to share the fruit of their VBS outreach to women. Beautiful new friendships were formed, and women were shown the love of Christ.

Is your church sharing space with another church? One church we attended provided meeting space for a Korean church. Though the sign in the front yard of the church was such a fixture that I rarely paid it much attention, one day the Lord got my attention. *Are we inviting these women to join us for our women's Bible study and women's ministry events?* A short discussion with the team and an email later, and we made that very belated invitation. If language barriers are a concern, perhaps you're supposed to be part of the solution.

Ask God to open the eyes of your team to the mission field He wants your women to work in.

Ask God to open the eyes of your team to the mission field He wants your women to work in. Just as we overlooked the Korean church, Pastor Robby Gallaty points out, "The most overlooked mission fields are the ones we spend the most time in: our workplaces, our neighborhoods, and in the presence of our family members."[42]

Lord, open our eyes!

CREATIVE IDEAS FOR ADDING MISSIONS TO YOUR CALENDAR

What are some practical and easy ways to add service activities and missions-oriented projects to your ministry calendar? In addition to adding donation drives to a couple of women's ministry events each year, consider swapping out a craft activity for a service project. Instead of a holiday party for your women, host a holiday party for the residents at a nursing home – bring gifts for them rather than giving gifts to one another.

You could add thirty minutes to the first Bible study session of the month and complete a service project together. Rather than hosting Bible study in your church building, what if you met in women's homes throughout your community and invited neighbors to attend? Search Pinterest for a list of Random Acts of Kindness (RAOK or RAK) and plan a night of RAOK in teams meeting up for coffee and fellowship afterward.

Want more ideas? Here's a list to get you started.

58 Service Project Ideas

Craft, Cook, and Create

1. Take a meal to a widow, homebound member, single mom, or recent divorcée in your church.
2. Bake goodies, such as cupcakes, and deliver them to your local police or fire station.
3. Write letters or send cards to missionaries.
4. Gather to assemble no-sew fleece blankets for a local children's home or women's shelter.
5. Knit or crochet prayer shawls and lap blankets for church members and friends that are facing health challenges.
6. Sew some pillowcase dresses for children in another country.
7. Cut out shoes for Sole Hope.
8. Put together and distribute homeless bags.
9. Host a sandwich-making party and pass them out to the homeless.
10. Assemble and distribute blessing bags for women who need some encouragement.
11. Send college care packages.
12. Put together Sonshine Boxes or bags and bless women in your church or community.
13. Fill a freezer with meals for a new mom.
14. Create birthday bags for your local food pantry (birthday cake, hats, candles, balloons).
15. Paint and decorate the teacher's lounge at a struggling school.
16. Create a community garden.

17. Decorate the bathrooms at a local school with positive messages.
18. Provide a meal for families at your local Ronald McDonald House.

Donate and Shop with a Purpose

19. Donate food to a local food shelter.
20. Gather and donate toiletries, make-up, and new underwear for a local women's shelter or sex trafficking ministry.
21. Bless a children's hospital with fun Band-Aids.
22. Purchase presents for a local Angel Tree.
23. Sponsor a family at a local school for Christmas.
24. Pack and distribute Thanksgiving baskets (turkey, stuffing, mashed potatoes, canned veggies, cranberry sauce) for families in need.
25. Collect gently used clothes and donate them to a ministry in need.
26. Hold a diaper drive for your local pregnancy ministry.
27. Donate children's books and movies to a local children's hospital.
28. Fill backpacks with school supplies for a teacher or school.
29. Hold a book drive for a local elementary school in need.
30. Host a baby shower for a local pregnancy center to help them restock supplies for pregnant and new mothers.
31. Hold a clothing drive for a local clothes closet ministry – or start your own!
32. Gather hats, scarves, and gloves for elementary school students in need.
33. Plan an Operation Christmas Child packing party for your neighborhood, church, or Bible study group.

Random Acts of Kindness

34. Deliver bags of groceries, firewood, or gift cards to a local family in need.
35. Tape quarters or dollar bills to the vending machines in the waiting room of your local hospital.

36. Leave quarters and washing detergent at your local laundry mat.
37. Pass out water bottles to construction workers on a hot day.
38. Leave bottles of bubbles at the park for families to use.
39. Host a block party in a community near your church.
40. Purchase coloring books and crayons and leave them in hospital waiting rooms or urgent care.

Volunteer Your Time

41. Volunteer to clean and organize at your local food shelter.
42. Work a shift at the local soup kitchen.
43. Find a local field or farm that allows folks to glean.
44. Volunteer at a local women's shelter, homeless shelter, or another ministry in need.
45. Clean the home of an elderly person or homebound member of your church.
46. Take care of some yard work or handyman chores for one of the widows in your church.
47. Volunteer to help a refugee family complete paperwork, register for school, etc.
48. Adopt a classroom at a school with low student test scores.
49. Visit a nursing home and host a game of bingo.
50. Christmas carol at a nursing home or children's hospital.
51. Cheer at a Special Olympics or special needs sports event.
52. Take on a Meals on Wheels route.
53. Plan a Habitat for Humanity workday.
54. Organize a free car care clinic for single moms in your community.
55. Clean the roadside – consider adopting a highway near your church.
56. Add some beauty and fresh landscaping to a school.
57. Take communion to homebound church members.
58. Organize a blood drive.

Don't just brainstorm among your team, ask your women where and how they'd like to serve! They may be aware of needs that you aren't, and they may even be willing to take the lead in coordinating the project.

A Few Words of Caution

I also want to offer a few words of caution. As authors Steve Corbett and Brian Fikkert state in the introduction of their book *When Helping Hurts: How to Alleviate Poverty Without Hurting the Poor . . . and Yourself,* "When North American Christians *do* attempt to alleviate poverty, the methods used often do considerable harm to both the materially poor and the materially non-poor. Our concern is not just that these methods are wasting human, spiritual, financial, and organizational resources but that these methods are actually exacerbating the very problems they are trying to solve."[43] Corbett and Fikkert advise, "A first helpful step in thinking about working with the poor in any context is to discern whether the situation calls for relief, rehabilitation, or development. In fact, the failure to distinguish among these situations is one of the most common reasons that poverty-alleviation efforts often do harm."[44]

Check to make sure the parachurch ministry has a plan in place to help the people they are serving move from crisis to self-sufficiency.

We have to take great care that our missions projects and activities help and don't harm those we work with. Will your donations take away income from a local store owner? Does your construction project prevent locals from working and earning a wage? Are you providing training that is needed and profitable? Is there a process in place to follow up or continue contact? Are your donations really wanted or needed?

Research the parachurch ministries you are considering partnering with to make sure they have a plan in place, not just for relief, but rehabilitation and development to help the people they are serving move from crisis to self-sufficiency.

Things to keep in mind as you prayerfully select a service or missions project:

- Take care that the way you collect donations allows for women in all financial positions to participate if they wish. No uncomfortable basket passing, please. Be grateful for donations of every size.
- Make sure your pastoral staff approves the project. Graciously accept their recommendations and direction.
- Open up the delivery of the donations to all of the women that came to the event (if possible). Your team should not be the only ones getting to participate in the blessing!

Be intentional with your missions projects. We want people to see Christ, not us.

The Challenge

What is God's desire for your women? Is He asking you to provide practical help and meet the physical needs of a ministry or community? Or is He asking you to go into the community, love your neighbors, share the gospel, and build relationships? While one-and-done projects are worthwhile and much needed, we also need to make sure we involve our women in local missions work that builds relationship. Imagine the impact your women could make with their consistent presence and participation with just one ministry partner or neighborhood!

Prayer

Lord, show us who and where You want our women to serve. Amen.

PRAYER POINTS: WHAT IS GOD PROMPTING ME TO MAKE A MATTER OF PRAYER?

PP

_____
_____
_____
_____
_____
_____
_____
_____

ACTION ITEMS: LIST THOSE THINGS UPON WHICH YOU SENSE GOD IS PROMPTING YOU TO TAKE ACTION.

AI

_____
_____
_____
_____
_____
_____
_____

Chapter 10

Rethinking Your Calendar

*And let us consider how we may spur one another on toward
love and good deeds, not giving up meeting together, as some
are in the habit of doing, but encouraging one another—
and all the more as you see the Day approaching.*
—Hebrews 10:24–25

HOW OFTEN SHOULD WE GATHER? IT'S one of the biggest questions women's ministry leaders struggle with. Leaders with small teams worry, rightfully so, about overtaxing their team members. How often is too often? How much is not enough?

There's no one-size-fits-all magical formula, but you can craft a plan that is best for your ministry in your church. Church attendance, precedent, team size, the church calendar, and the Lord's leading must all be taken into consideration. Resist the urge to copy the calendar of the women's ministry at another church.

If you're starting from scratch or relaunching a women's ministry, you may not have a precedent to follow or years of expectations that must be taken into account. As your team grows and God expands your ministry reach, you can add more events and activities to your calendar. It's okay to start slow, and it's much better than burning your team out fast!

If you're an established women's ministry team, it may be that God is asking you to rethink your current women's ministry offerings.

Are your offerings a bit out of balance? Are there holes in your calendar the Lord wants you to fill? Are there some things you need to press pause on for the next year – or for a season? Have you neglected working women by offering most of your events during the daytime? Does your calendar look the same as it did five years ago? It's unlikely a big overhaul is required, but some tweaking here and there might better serve your women. Let's prayerfully explore what, if any, changes God may be asking you to consider. (Side note: We'll work through how to make those changes in chapter 13.)

You can craft a plan that is best for your ministry in your church.

It can be tempting to plan one event or activity at a time, waiting until the event is over to plan the next thing. Despite the temptation to be laser focused on the current event, there are a few flaws with that approach.

- Your team should always have an invitation to extend at the end of every event. What is coming next? When can women connect again?
- You risk losing momentum. Your women need to connect regularly to build and deepen relationships. Don't make them wait long periods between events or activities.
- You're at the mercy of the church calendar. When it comes to securing dates for events, the early bird gets the worm! You may find there are few available or preferable dates left on the church calendar for your next event.

Most teams find that securing dates on the calendar six months or a year in advance works best. You may want to distribute save-the-date cards to your women with the events, times, and dates for the next six months. This allows them to plan ahead and gives your team the flexibility to make some changes, if necessary, to those events that are farther out in the future. If God places an opportunity in your path, you can always add to the calendar if needed.

How Many Events Should We Host?

One women's ministry leader told me her pastor only allows them to host two women's ministry events per year. That's hard. It's difficult to build connections and deepen relationships when we only see each other a couple of times a year. I recommend, at minimum, you host four events per year. Try to equally space them throughout the calendar year. If our women have to miss an event, we don't want them to have to wait months for another!

Not every event, though, needs to be a big event. If we look at Jesus's ministry, we'll see that He ministered to people on three different scales. In Matthew 5, we see Jesus teaching to large crowds. For example, Matthew 14:13–21 highlights Jesus's feeding five thousand people and Matthew 15:29–39 records Him feeding a crowd of four thousand. Like Jesus, we should host events for large groups. I recommend small to large churches (up to two thousand in weekend attendance) plan one big event per year, such as a retreat, special event, or conference. These big events might include women from other churches and almost always work best with six months to one year for planning with a separate planning team.

Jesus also ministered to smaller crowds. Matthew 4:23 tells us, "Jesus went throughout Galilee, teaching in their synagogues, proclaiming the good news of the kingdom, and healing every disease and sickness among the people." We should also host medium-sized events, ones that all women are invited to attend, but which don't require the large-scale planning of a big event. Medium-sized events include worship nights, special speakers, workshops, paint nights, game nights, movie nights, service projects, or dinner out. There's still some prep work required, but you may not need a separate planning team.

Jesus also ministered to more intimate, small groups. He frequently gathered with the twelve disciples (see Mark 3:14–19) and often with His team of three: Peter, James, and John (see Mark 9:2 and Mark 14:33). We, too, should offer smaller group opportunities for our women. Bible study or discipleship groups encourage smaller groups of women to gather together. In-home events, such as potluck dinners, movies, or game nights, create opportunities for greater connection and intimacy.

Your church size will determine the number of large, medium, and small events you host. In a small church, all of your events may be geared toward small groups because you're still growing! In a large or megachurch (two thousand people or more), you're going to want to create opportunities for women to gather in different group sizes. And even within those big events, we want to allow women opportunities to gather in smaller groups.

As you schedule events on your calendar, consider the expected attendance of your event and space them out accordingly. In addition, you'll also want to vary the types of events you offer, but we'll dig into that in the next chapter!

SELECTING THE BEST DATE FOR AN EVENT

Picking the best date for your women's ministry event can be tricky. While throwing a dart at a calendar may seem tempting, we can do better than that! Admittedly, there is no perfect date that will meet the needs of every woman in your church, but we can eliminate some poor choices.

We're going to attack this backward. We need to eliminate those dates that won't work first, and it's all about eliminating the competition. Don't give your women an easy excuse not to attend.

Let's take a look at events, groups, and activities that might cause a conflict:

- Don't compete against other ministries: senior ministry, youth ministry, choir.
- Don't compete with large church event such as VBS or a Christmas program (includes setup and rehearsals).
- Be mindful of school vacation days and keep a copy of the school calendar; know which school/school districts your students attend. Pay attention to open house nights too.

- Schedule around and not on holidays; even if the event is for Valentine's or Mother's Day choose a different day.
- Avoid regular community activities such as craft fairs, Friday night football games, or a balloon festival.
- Consider sports schedules; if your city is home to an NFL stadium, don't plan an event at the same time and day as a home game.

Women are busy... we can make their choice easier by scheduling events when we know there will be fewer conflicts.

It isn't going to be possible to eliminate every potential conflict. Women are busy, and they will have to choose to come. However, we can make that choice easier by scheduling events when we know there will be fewer conflicts.

Additional calendar tips:

- If your church calendar isn't available online, ask your church secretary to send you a copy before your women's ministry meeting.
- Try to schedule events on different days of the week (unless it's a recurring event). If one of your women always works the Friday night shift at the hospital, she'll never be able to attend if you only hold events on Friday nights.
- May and December are especially tricky; Mother's Day and college and high school graduations will eliminate most weekends in May. December is often filled with church events and Christmas parties; early in the month or even late November may work better.

Before you place an event on the calendar, ask your team these three questions:

1. Have you checked the church calendar?
2. Have you checked the school calendar?
3. What events might we be competing with?

ACCOUNT FOR PLANNING TIME

Bigger events usually require more planning time. Are you going to assemble a planning team? Will you need to search for a speaker? Will you need to secure a venue or a catering company? If you're booking a well-known speaker, you may need to secure the date more than a year in advance. Planning teams will need about six to nine months of lead time to organize an event with excellence. While some people claim they work best under pressure, we want to avoid creating a stressful planning situation. We want our planning team members to share their excitement about the event with other women, not their complaints about how stressful or hurried the planning process has been.

God doesn't rush or hurry. He has a plan, and nothing He does is by accident. I try to remember these truths when event planning starts to feel forced. The Lord is also quick to remind me what happened when we tried to plan a retreat in fewer than four months.

Several summers ago, the women's ministry team I was serving on had to decide whether or not to continue with plans for a fall retreat. We were without a location, theme, budget, and date with about four months to pull all the details together. Returning to the previously used retreat location was not an option as we needed dedicated meeting space. Our team was divided on whether or not we should move forward. I volunteered to research possible retreat locations for availability and cost, well aware that many of our team members were in for a shock. The previous year they had received a crazy great deal. Based on my previous experience booking retreat and conference centers, I was confident the market rate for two nights and five meals was going to be significantly higher.

As we met and debated our options, some members of our team grew more and more uncomfortable. There was pushback against the higher cost. We hadn't yet landed on a verse or theme that everyone agreed on. Some team members began to push and panic. If we were going to have our retreat that fall, we had to get stuff done now! There was a hurriedness about our approach that didn't seem right. Could

RETHINKING YOUR CALENDAR | 133

we pull it off? Sure! But was that the best option for our women or our team? Probably not.

After much prayer, phone calls, and some rather emotional conversations, we were finally able to come to a unanimous decision to host the retreat the next year when we could take the time needed to make plans. Though everyone was not pleased, everyone agreed it was the right decision. God had several reasons for taking us through that decision-making process. Our research into retreat locations had done two great things.

1. We narrowed down our list of preferred retreat locations.
2. We discovered that most retreat venues book one year in advance.

Waiting a year gave us time to tour our top picks and more easily secure a date. Working through conflict was good for our team. We were able to move forward united and confident that God used the *no* in that season for a *yes* in the next.

Should You Cancel?

Your event has been on the calendar for months, but sign-ups so far are disappointing, and you're beginning to wonder is it even worth it. Almost every leader has wrestled with what to do when it doesn't look as if there will be many women attending. You wonder, *Should we cancel?*

I'm assuming you prayed about this event before ever putting it on your church calendar, right?

God knew in advance who would and would not show up. Our job is to be obedient and to carry out the tasks He's given us.

God knew in advance who would and would not show up. Our job is to be obedient and to carry out the tasks He's given us. I know this can be difficult when the numbers on paper cause us to panic.

Keep in mind:

- Women are notoriously slow to sign up for women's ministry events. Keep working every publicity angle and trust the numbers will come.
- Sometimes God is calling you or your team to have faith and trust Him with the outcome.
- It isn't about the numbers. Sometimes it's about the one.
- Turn your panic into prayers. Maybe your team needs to be on their knees, praying for women to register.
- There are women who can't wait!

If you're tempted to cancel, please consider the women who will be disappointed if you do. After one of our moves, I signed up to attend an *After the Boxes Are Unpacked* book club for women who were new to the area. I couldn't wait for our first meeting! I was struggling, and I knew these women would understand. But instead of sympathetic hugs, I got the call that there wasn't enough interest. I wouldn't have cared if it was just three of us. I was so lonely and desperate to connect. I took the snub personally and let my husband know that was one church we wouldn't be visiting. While I hope and pray not one single woman will take your cancellation personally, be aware it can happen.

I have been so encouraged by leaders who have shared about the divine appointments and sweet times of prayer and encouragement they've had when only one or two women showed up. Don't miss those moments! Embrace the opportunity God has given you. Show those one or two women that they are valuable, and they are loved. God brought them there for a reason.

So is it ever okay to cancel? You should only cancel an event if:

- Your pastor asks you to. Kindly ask questions if necessary but submit to authority (Hebrews 13:17).
- The weather makes travel dangerous. Make sure your women know how you'll communicate any weather-related cancellations.

- Continuing with the event would be a financial burden to the church; get input from the pastoral staff and treasurer before making this call yourself. There may be funds you are unaware of, or grace may be extended and a budget shortfall allowed.

If you do have to cancel:

- Quickly confer with your team and enlist their help in communicating the cancelation.
- Use every communication means possible to spread the word – phone, text, email, Facebook, website, etc. Hang a sign on the church doors if at all possible.
- Refund any money if you can. If you cannot issue refunds, make sure you state that when women register.
- Cancel promptly, but not too early. Here in the South, predictions and actual snowfall can vary widely. A forecast a week out would never be a reason to cancel.
- Consider rescheduling. Depending upon the type of event and the anticipated attendance, you may wish to reschedule.

Frequently communicate your weather cancellation plan if cancellations are common in the area where you live. One Bible study group I attended had the policy that if the city schools were closed, we would not meet. They always followed up with a reminder when we did have to cancel, but at least it wasn't a surprise.

Should You Take a Summer Sabbatical?

If you normally take a summer ministry break, I want to encourage you to rethink your decision. I know it can be tempting to give your team and your women a break over the summer, but it may not be what's best for your team or your women. I have yet to come across a verse in the Bible that recommends a summer siesta from all things church, but we often act as if it does. Taking a summer break gives our women permission to dial back their Bible study time, church attendance, and involvement.

I didn't believe there would be much interest in a summer Bible study until I experienced it firsthand. I wrongly assumed that women would want to take a summer break, but instead discovered summer studies often reached a different group of women. Some of our Bible study faithful attended, but we also had a large group of teachers who were thrilled that summer break allowed them to participate in a daytime Bible study.

As you host summer women's ministry events, you will find moms will thank you for a break from all-day efforts of keeping their kids busy. Slower summer schedules actually leave room for women to attend women's ministry events and activities. Also, when other church ministries take a summer sabbatical, there is less on the church calendar to compete with. And those who are new to your church will be thrilled that they can get connected quickly.

Summer breaks have the potential to greatly weaken or kill your ministry momentum.

Summer breaks have the potential to greatly weaken or kill your ministry momentum. Many of your women rely on the Bible studies to keep them accountable and in the Word. Your women look forward to regularly connecting with other women in the church.

Another summer bonus is the opportunity to change things up a bit and test-drive new ideas. Our current church offers summer book clubs throughout June, July, and August. Some churches offer shorter Bible studies. Consider hosting a lake day or summer salads supper, attending an outdoor concert, going kayaking, or offering an ice cream social. Invite women to participate in VBS for adults, take a mission trip, host a block party at a nearby apartment complex, or hand out popsicles in a neighborhood next to the church. Embrace the opportunities summer months can bring.

Women need Jesus every single day of the year. When we stop our activities in mid-May and break until early September, that's easily sixteen weeks without offering women the chance to study, fellowship, grow, and build relationships with each other.

While we shouldn't press pause on summer ministry activities, we also shouldn't take a break from our women's ministry team meetings – though it can be tempting! When our women's ministry team failed to meet one summer, it negatively impacted our biggest event of the year. Email and phone calls were not sufficient. We were short on time, and our planning was rushed. Our registration team took the biggest hit because there wasn't time for sufficient training. It also put pressure on our church staff when it came to publicizing the event. A summer meeting would have made a huge difference! If you are planning a fall women's ministry event of any kind, you definitely need to meet during the summer.

Prayer

God, please give us wisdom and discernment as we create our women's ministry calendars. May the dates we choose and the activities we plan complement, and not compete with, other church events or ministries. Help us to serve and show love to every woman that comes. Amen.

PRAYER POINTS: WHAT IS GOD PROMPTING ME TO MAKE A MATTER OF PRAYER?

PP

_____

_____

_____

_____

_____

_____

_____

ACTION ITEMS: LIST THOSE THINGS UPON WHICH YOU SENSE GOD IS PROMPTING YOU TO TAKE ACTION.

AI

_____

_____

_____

_____

_____

_____

_____

Chapter 11

Rethinking Women's Ministry Events

*They devoted themselves to the apostles' teaching and to
fellowship, to the breaking of bread and to prayer.*
—Acts 2:42

HAT DO WOMEN REALLY THINK ABOUT women's ministry
events? Here's just a small sample of comments from the
women's ministry survey I conducted:

*"I feel like they go out of their way to be extra feminine...i.e.,
décor, topics. Just be normal."*

*"I will never attend another fluffy tea party or spring mother/
daughter type event with little to no spiritual nourishment. I
despise this form of 'ministry' and feel it serves no purpose."*

*"Cliques, focus on décor, shiny things, pomp and circum-
stance. I love things simple, pretty, and focused on Christ, not
the color of the tablecloth."*

*"Goofy women's events: I don't want to dress up in a poodle
skirt and pretend to be a teen. Or wear 'pink' boas and play
children's games. I'm 55, not 12. If I was doing it in children's
ministry that would be different."*

"Boring."

*"Primary focus on 'fun' and 'fluff' in order to attract atten-
dance - everyone's time is valuable, everyone is busy, and her
time should not be wasted on events that don't spur growth
and change."*

Ouch! I wish I could report that these comments were the
exception and not the rule, but I can't. Over and over again, women
repeatedly commented about over-the-top, ultra-feminine décor.
They are tired of events that lack depth and purpose. It's no wonder
we're struggling to get women to show up!

Before you dismiss these comments as relevant only to other
women's ministries at other churches, let me ask you a few hard questions (ones I've wrestled with myself):

- Does your team spend more time decorating for an event than
  praying as a group for your event?
- If you have a speaker, how much of the schedule is dedicated
  to the message?
- When women talk about your events, what's the first thing
  they mention? Is it the décor?
- Do women bring a Bible to your events without prompting or
  reminders?

I'm concerned there's often a disconnect between the events
many women's ministry teams offer and the wants and needs of our
women. Steeped in years of tradition, our senior saints look forward
to the annual tea and table events. Yet, a glance around the room
often reveals multiple generations are missing from the festivities. It's
important that we regularly assess the reach and effectiveness of our
women's ministry events.

While there is nothing wrong or unbiblical about tea parties and
pink decorations, if our events lack depth and fail to spur the spiritual
growth of our women, we have done them a great disservice. It's easy
to get distracted by checklists, food choices, and pretty decorations
and miss the purpose of our women's ministry events.

I'll never forget the first year I experienced the annual table event.
Fairly new to the church and a co-leader for mere weeks, this event

was eye-opening. I was eager to listen to the speaker my co-leader had chosen (before I joined the team). She had an amazing story to share, and I knew the women would be in awe of what God had done in her life since her husband's sudden and tragic death.

As we went over the setup schedule for the event, I had a lot of questions. There was, what seemed to me, an excessive amount of time set aside for the table hostesses to come in and set up their tables. *Did they really need that much time?* I soon found out, yes, indeed they did. Most of the hostesses went to elaborate lengths to decorate their tables; several of whom had been planning their décor and table theme from the moment last year's event ended.

If our events lack depth and fail to spur the spiritual growth of our women, we have done them a great disservice.

Women were known for showing up almost thirty minutes before the doors were set to open, and they didn't disappoint! There was no holding them back. They couldn't wait to get inside and admire all of the beautiful tablescapes. I was thrilled to see such excitement for our biggest event of the year! Things seemed to be flowing smoothly, and the women were engaged and attentive for the first ten minutes that our speaker spoke. My first red flag was that hardly anyone (no one I could see anyway) had brought their Bible or was taking any notes. I tried to squash my concerns so I could focus on our speaker's message; it was just as powerful and as moving as I had expected. As we were cleaning up after the event, I heard women were complaining about how long the speaker spoke. Unbeknown to them, she had finished ten minutes early! It seems they were expecting a shorter and lighter message.

As is evident in the example above, different types of women's ministry events attract different women in your church. That's actually a good thing! As we refine our ministry strategy, we need to strive to consistently offer different types of events so we can extend our reach. As we draw women in through an event that speaks to their ministry language, we can then invite them to go deeper with us to experience growth and transformation. Bible studies should not be the only place women find deep teaching and God's Word.

DIFFERENT TYPES OF WOMEN'S MINISTRY EVENTS

I am so thankful God gives us rein to minister to women in all sorts of creative ways! Offering different types of women's ministry events is one way to try to meet those needs better. Meeting the needs of so many different women isn't an easy task, but it isn't impossible either. Offering a variety of women's ministry events ensures we meet the different needs of our women, keeps our ministry from becoming stale, and creates a more balanced schedule.

You may find it helpful to categorize the types of events your team offers. A quick tally might reveal your offerings are a bit heavy on fellowship and lacking in developing the spiritual disciplines. Or you may find the opposite is true, your offerings are more often deep than not, providing few entry points for women who are not believers or are new Christians.

I've broken down the different types of women's ministry events into five categories:

1. Spiritual disciplines
2. Biblical encouragement
3. Practical skills
4. Service
5. Fellowship focused

Here's a quick description of each, as well as examples of events that may fall into that category.

1. **Spiritual disciplines** – Women learn, experience, and practice a spiritual discipline. Prayer, worship, meditation, fasting, journaling, Bible study, and evangelism all fall under this umbrella. Possible event ideas include Bible journaling, prayer, How to Study the Bible, How to Honor the Sabbath, Worship and Prayer Night, and How to Share Jesus. Both in-house and professional speakers can be used to

deliver the content. Include time for your women to apply and practice what they have learned.

2. **Biblical encouragement** - Women are encouraged by a teaching or testimony that highlights God's faithfulness and presence. God's Word is central to the message, and application of biblical truth is encouraged. Examples of events offering biblical encouragement include guest speakers, personal testimonies, speaker panels, and topical teachings.

Consider hosting a series of talks on "taboo topics" such as sexual identity, abortion, pornography, sexual abuse, addiction, and mental health. Counter the teaching of the culture with God's Word on each topic.

Sharing stories of hope and healing offers encouragement, but great care needs to be taken to keep the focus on spiritual transformation and Christ rather than emotions and the flesh. Consider asking your speaker for an outline of their talk.

3. **Practical skills** – Women learn, experience, and practice a practical skill. Survey your women to uncover the skills they'd like to learn. You may have women in your church that can teach these skills, or you may need to find a professional from the community. Examples of practical skills events include painting parties, organizing, fashion tips, flower arranging, knitting, chalk paint techniques, budgeting, canning, making jam, marriage workshops, meal planning, and parenting workshops. Events that focus on a practical skill are often optimal outreach events.

Whenever possible, content should be framed through the lens of the Bible.

Whenever possible, content should be framed through the lens of the Bible. An easy way to add the gospel to a skill-based event is to have a woman share a testimony that ties in with the topic. For example, someone may have a relative that canned fruits and vegetables who also encouraged their faith. Another way to link the Bible to a skill-based event is to have a short lesson on what the Bible has to say about the topic. What does the Bible say about budgeting? What does the Bible say about being a good steward?

4.   **Service** – While we want to encourage our women to serve in the community, offering opportunities at the church that connect women to the community are also beneficial. Invite a ministry partner to share briefly about what they do and conclude your time with a hands-on project that will support that ministry in a meaningful way. Ideas include sandwiches for the local homeless ministry, no-sew fleece blankets for the women's shelter, pillowcase dresses to send with those going on a mission trip, notecards for local teachers, and cupcakes for emergency responders.

5.   **Fellowship focused** – This may be the type of event you assume is the most popular based on past attendance. It may even be tempting to offer more fellowship-focused events than others, but I want to discourage you from doing so. Offering too many fellowship-focused events could very easily water down your mission: to share Christ and spur spiritual growth in your women. Fellowship-focused events should be sprinkled lightly throughout your schedule, not applied liberally. Women repeatedly told me when surveyed that they want depth, not just a social event.

Offering too many fellowship-focused events could very easily water down your mission: to share Christ and spur spiritual growth in your women.

Fellowship-focused events include game nights, potlucks, table events, holiday celebrations, and movie nights. Fellowship-focused events might appear secular at first glance but should always point women to the gospel. Sharing a testimony is an easy way to encourage women at these events to remind them of the hope and freedom that can be found in Christ.

It's quite possible your event may not fit neatly into one of the categories above. Maybe it's a combination. That's okay! The goal is not to offer one of each type of event each quarter or every other month.

We're not striving for an equal balance of different women's ministry event types, but we are striving for a variety.

At the beginning of this chapter, I highlighted what women *don't* want at women's ministry events; here's what they *do* want. Check out these comments from the women's ministry survey:

> *"It needs to be a warm, friendly environment where women can be vulnerable and where Scripture is taught and applied to our hearts."*

> *"It must be spiritually inspiring, focused on pointing us to Jesus, and then growing us in the Word. It must be joyful and loving. I must feel welcome and valued."*

> *"It is important that the Word of God is handled and presented accurately. It is also important that the atmosphere is loving and all inclusive."*

> *"That it be welcoming to all women no matter where they are in their spiritual journey."*

> *'That the topic is presented intellectually and with gospel-centered/grace-based applications. Often, women's ministry scratches the surface of being intellectually stimulating or academic but is very heartfelt. It would be nice to have both present and coexisting."*

> *"The event should be fun and engaging with activities that all ages can enjoy. I want those in attendance to leave the event with a desire to draw closer to the Lord."*

Four Secrets to Great Women's Ministry Events

How do we create events that reflect those needs mentioned above? These four secrets provide the reminders your team may need:

1. God and Christ must be the cornerstone of every event.

God knows exactly what the women in your specific church need, but it is important to take the time to uncover it through time in prayer and His Word. Before you search Google or scroll through Pinterest, seek the Lord's will. Can He use an event idea you've plucked from Pinterest or purchased in a box? Sure, He's God! But I can promise you His ideas are always better than our own.

We must include Jesus at every event. Pointing women to Christ and encouraging their spiritual growth should both be a part of your mission statement in some form. As you set your calendar, use your mission statement and your theme Scripture as a plumb line for each event and activity. Ask your team members as they make suggestions, "How does that event idea support our mission and encompass our theme for this year?"

Every event should always be anchored with a Scripture verse or passage, no matter what type of women's ministry event you have planned. Anchoring your event with God's Word points women to Christ, communicates the importance of Scripture, and reminds your women to view the event or activity through the lens of the Bible.

If your team is struggling to find a way to connect your event topic with God's Word, that's a red flag. Take time to examine the lack of connection and make any needed changes.

2. Our focus must be on spiritual transformation.

Our heart's desire is for our women to become more like Christ. We can encourage that process by creating and offering events that offer an encounter with Jesus and encourage transformation.

Whether we intend to or not, creating events that intentionally elicit an emotional response from our women is manipulative. Feelings, though powerful, can be deceptive. We want God to transform the hearts of our women. Feelings ebb and flow. Our women need to learn to operate in the truth of God's Word and by the power of the Holy Spirit, often in spite of what they feel.

Our heart's desire is for our women to become more like Christ. We can encourage that process by creating and offering events that offer an encounter with Jesus and encourage transformation.

Ephesians 4:22–24 encourages us to put off the old self and put on the new. Our women should be changing and growing! We may not always see new growth, but we have a responsibility to plant seeds and water them.

Always ask your team, how will women encounter Christ? Answer the question before and after the event. Reflecting on how you saw God at work in your post-event evaluation (see the free bonus materials online for a copy of the "Post-Event Evaluation Form") will keep your team focused on prioritizing God's Word and on opportunities for spiritual growth.

3. We must create an engaging and interactive plan for our events.

The best women's ministry events are interactive. As you plan your event, make sure you provide something for your women to do beyond grabbing a plate of food and participating in an icebreaker. Get them up out of their seats and moving around the room.

Ask them to:

- Complete a task
- Write down a response
- Discuss the topic at their table
- Participate in a project
- Offer a response
- Make or do something with their hands

Long lectures without discussion or interaction may discourage your women from returning. Placing your women in circles, and not rows, will naturally encourage discussion and connection. Provide an opportunity for your women to apply and practice what they have learned. Women don't just want to listen; they want to do!

We must include a time for women to discuss what it is they have heard or experienced. Discussion solidifies and internalizes the message. We need to encourage our women to think about the message and what action God may be prompting them to take in response. When we share those thoughts with others, suddenly there is accountability!

Our women become more comfortable sharing what God is doing in their lives by talking about what God is doing in their lives.

Consider using these three questions for the discussion groups at your next event:

- What did you hear that challenged you?
- What did you hear that reinforced a teaching from the Bible?
- What action do you feel God wants you to take in response?

4. Every event or activity should be delivered with excellence.

Sometimes we confuse fancy decorations and theme-infused presentations with excellence. Women are not judging your craft skills; they are measuring the depth of your teaching and thoroughness of preparation. Women were not too shy in their survey responses to point out that they've been to events that were unorganized and lacking in purpose.

I'll never forget the retreat I attended where the women's ministry leader apologized. She admitted that they had thrown things together at the last minute. Unfortunately, that explained a lot. There was no excuse for her lack of planning. She failed to put a retreat planning team together. She hadn't asked for help.

Time plus intentionality will yield an awesome event!

Organization adds the polish to an event that will leave your women feeling valued and treasured. Take the time to figure out how long each piece of your event requires and do your best to stick to the schedule. Recruit volunteers to execute necessary tasks. Prep your materials. Tap your type-A girls to work through the details so nothing is forgotten. Handpick the person who will be doing most of the speaking. Enthusiasm and a sense of humor will help encourage your women to open up and participate. Time plus intentionality will yield an awesome event!

EVENT CHECKLIST

As you review your event agenda, check to make sure you've included:

- Prayer – at the minimum an opening and closing prayer.

- Announcements – present other opportunities for your women.
- Icebreaker – this provides an opportunity for women to connect, develop deeper relationships, and interact with women in the room they may not know or may not know well.
- Testimony – we need our women to share stories about what God is teaching them or doing in their lives.
- Teaching – related to the theme or spiritual focus, or activity directions
- Interaction – either through a planned activity (craft, service project, skill, workshop) or small discussion groups.

You may need to tweak this checklist based on the amount of time allotted for your event. Weekly women's ministry events that meet at the same time as other ministry activities may require your team to work within the hour or so that you've been given. In that case, you may want to email your announcements and alternate an icebreaker with a testimony each week. Your focus may be on weekly teachings with a monthly or quarterly break for a service project.

Two hours is usually sufficient for most monthly or quarterly events. Conferences and retreats will, of course, require additional time. Any shorter, and women won't feel it's worth their time to get ready and leave their home. Much longer, and women may struggle to find space in an already tight schedule. It's better they leave wishing they'd had another hour together than wishing the event had ended sooner!

Door Prizes and Food

In some churches, food and door prizes at a women's ministry event are expected. If door prizes or food have become a distraction at your events, I am giving you permission to remove them. Read the chapter on sacred cows before making any drastic changes, though, please.

If your budget allows, door prizes that point women toward Christ can be nice and even promote spiritual growth, but they are not necessary. Christian movie DVDs, water bottles with a Scripture verse, trusted Christian books, verses on plaques, and pretty journals can be placed in a door prize basket so women can choose a door prize they want and will use. I try to keep the cost of each door prize to around five dollars so everyone feels they are receiving something equal in value. Expensive or elaborate door prizes distract from the event and can be the source of jealousy among your women.

Food is not a necessity and often wreaks havoc on an already tight schedule. I've noticed several churches asking women to arrive early or stay late to enjoy snacks outside of the main event space. For example, invite women to arrive 6:30 p.m. for a cupcake bar in the lobby before the event begins at 7:00 p.m. Food-focused events can also deter women with food allergies and diet restrictions from attending. If at all possible, please make accommodations for those women when you can. While they may be used to not being able to eat out, the option to eat safe food will bless them.

I'm continually amazed in our Facebook group by the creative ways women's ministry teams use their God-given gifts to create events that point women toward Christ. Encourage creativity, while holding your team to your purpose, and your ministry and women will be blessed!

Prayer

Lord, show us where we may need to make some adjustments in our event planning. If there's a need we're failing to meet, please show us clearly what it is and how to meet it. Help us to plan events that will draw our women into a deeper relationship with You and each other. Amen.

PRAYER POINTS: WHAT IS GOD PROMPTING ME TO MAKE A MATTER OF PRAYER?

PP

_____

_____

_____

_____

_____

_____

_____

ACTION ITEMS: LIST THOSE THINGS UPON WHICH YOU SENSE GOD IS PROMPTING YOU TO TAKE ACTION.

AI

_____

_____

_____

_____

_____

_____

_____

Chapter 12

Rethinking Publicity

But blessed are your eyes because they see,
and your ears because they hear.
—Matthew 13:16

GONE ARE THE DAYS WHEN PAPER women's ministry newsletters and flyers in the bathroom stall were the best and often only necessary publicity for women's ministry events. Modern technology requires we cast our nets wide. In this chapter, we'll dig into the how, what, and where of creating publicity that will reach your women and encourage their participation.

We live in a visual world, and creating publicity that connects with your women will impact your reach. You may need to recruit a women's ministry team member whose task is to create publicity. We want to do it well and do it right.

We may think our past publicity efforts have been sufficient, but time and time again I hear from women who had no idea an event or activity was taking place, despite the efforts our team had made! It can be downright frustrating! You may be familiar with the marketing "rule of seven" in which prospects need to come across an offer at least seven times before they notice it and will start to take action. As marketing expert Kathi Kruse notes, "You might need more than those seven times just to be heard above all the clutter that's in people's Newsfeeds or fields of vision."[45] We want to present our information early and often.

Do Your Women Know They Are Invited?

In addition to sharing our message consistently, we also need to make certain it's connecting to our target audience. Do women of all ages and stages know the event is for them? Ministry names can sometimes create more confusion and lack clarity. For months I saw announcements for events and activities for the J.O.Y. (Just Older Youth) group. I assumed the group was for college students and young professionals since they were now too old for youth group. I was quite surprised to discover that the J.O.Y. group was actually the name for the senior adult ministry. While I still wasn't the target audience, I tucked that lesson away as a reminder to make clear the intended target as I craft publicity pieces. Creative ministry names can be fun, but they also require explanation.

In addition to sharing our message consistently, we also need to make certain it's connecting to our target audience.

Speaking of invitations, personal invites trump traditional publicity methods every single time. Several years ago, our women's ministry team received some rather frustrating feedback on a survey. One of the women noted that she had never attended a women's ministry event because she had never been invited. *Seriously?!* Some of the members on our team couldn't believe her comment, as they viewed every piece of publicity as an open invitation. It was a personal invitation that she must have desired. Though we disagreed with her comment to a point, our team became more intentional about making personal invites to our activities and events. We also started including the words "you are invited" in publicity pieces.

WHERE TO PUBLICIZE YOUR EVENTS

Figuring out what will work with your group of women may feel like throwing spaghetti at a wall to see what sticks. Rather than posting on every social media app and plastering posters on every church wall, let's craft a strategy. The very first thing you need to do is figure out where your women are hanging out online as well as physically inside your church building (if you have one).

You should be able to easily observe the traffic patterns of the women in your church and position publicity materials in their path. Yes, putting flyers in the bathroom still works! Please make sure you obtain the proper approvals (staff and building and grounds) before displaying any new publicity in your church.

Here's a list of twenty-five ways to distribute publicity inside your church. Don't panic – you won't need to use all of them for every event or activity. Decide as a team which will be most effective.

1. Sunday bulletins (multiple weeks, starting three or four weeks prior)
2. Bulletin boards
3. Registration forms
4. Videos
5. Bathroom flyers
6. Sunday school announcements
7. Sunday school folder flyers
8. Pulpit announcements
9. Sandwich boards
10. Emails to attendees (not just members!)
11. Email newsletters
12. Church calendars
13. Announcements at events and Bible studies
14. Printed newsletters
15. Social Media (Facebook, Instagram, etc.)
16. Church signs (if you have one that is electronic or with change-able letters)
17. PowerPoint announcement slides before service begins

18. Save-the-date cards
19. Personal invitations
20. Bulletin inserts (bookmarks, flyers)
21. Postcards mailed to attendees
22. Candy mini flyers
23. Banners
24. Registration tables
25. Church website

Online publicity may be a bigger challenge for your team. Not only will you need to create social media and other online postings, but you'll need to figure out where to put them. Periodically ask your women where they spend their time online. As new social media apps are created and as women enter new stages in life, their answers will change. Because social media usage usually varies by age, you'll need to target different social media channels to reach all of your women effectively. At this writing, Facebook is a better target for your women over forty, and Instagram will more likely reach your women under forty. I have not found Twitter to be effective for publicizing women's ministry events. Let your numbers determine your focus.

Women often visit virtually before attending their first women's ministry event. Creating an engaging, informative online presence is no longer optional. At a minimum, I suggest your team set up a web page on your church website and a closed Facebook group. I recommend closed Facebook groups because only group members can see the posts and they can be a powerful tool for building community. If you have the bandwidth to manage both a Facebook page and a closed Facebook group, by all means, go for it. Keep in mind, you'll need to post regularly to both. Your group will need admins to post information, approve new group members, monitor the conversation, and delete any posts that fail to stay within your group guidelines.

Algorithms, the mystical formula social media companies use to display and rank the items in your social media feed, are constantly changing. If you have a woman on your team that understands the best practices for postings on social media, regularly seek out her advice. Not every woman that follows your Instagram account or is a member of your Facebook group will see every single thing you post. You might post five times about an event, but Karen may only see two of those posts. Share more than you think you need to! Ask your team members to like, comment, and share your online content to help extend its visibility and reach.

WHAT TO INCLUDE IN YOUR PUBLICITY

Before we discuss creating publicity, let's look at what you need to include in your publicity. I can't tell you how many times I've failed to include a key piece of information. Always follow up in writing with the key details of your event for your team members. I distinctly remember opening up my Sunday morning bulletin at one church to discover that the start time listed was wrong for an event that our women's ministry team was hosting. When I followed up with the team member in charge of publicity, she thought it was accurate. In the grand scheme of things, it really wasn't a huge deal as the event time was only off by half an hour, but it did highlight the need to communicate details effectively among our team members and necessitated some tweaks to the event agenda.

Always follow up in writing with the key details of your event for your team members.

Always assume there will be new members and guests attending your event. The checklist below will ensure you share those details that we sometimes assume everyone knows.

- Name of the event *
- Location *
- Time *
- Date *
- Day of the week
- Cost *
- Childcare (cost, registration info, or not available)
- Registration information (if needed)

- A brief description of the event *
- Ministry logo
- Contact information (website, church office, email) *
- What they need to bring (Bible, donations, craft supplies, love offering)

*These things should be included in shorter publicity pieces where space is limited; include directions on how to find out more information.

Be sure to download the "Publicity Form" from the free bonus materials online.

How to Create Captivating Publicity

If you are blessed to have a women's ministry team member or a staff member that can create quality publicity materials and graphics for you, turn down the corner of this page and take a moment to send them a thank you note! Most women's ministry leaders are not so fortunate. Even if not, we can still create captivating publicity; it's just going to take a little more effort! Before selecting the DIY route, search among your women for someone with graphic design experience that can help. If that search isn't fruitful, we have two other options.

1. We can learn how to do it.
2. We can pay someone to do it.

Your budget and the significance of your event or activity will likely determine which of those two options is best. There are many online sites you can use to hire someone to create a flyer, registration form, or logo for your event. Closely examine their portfolio and be crystal clear about what you want to be created and at what price. Look for someone with excellent reviews who is willing to make unlimited changes and can complete the work in the needed timeframe.

Even if someone is helping you design your publicity, you'll want to keep the following information in mind as you communicate your preferences. Consistency is critical. If at all possible, the same person should write all copy, and the same person should design all of the graphics, posters, and flyers. You'll want to use the same wording, the same colors, and the same fonts across all publicity formats. Don't forget to double-check to make certain each piece of information is included.

Outdated publicity sends a clear message to your younger women – this isn't for you. If you are still creating flyers in Publisher templates that were created more than five years ago, your publicity probably looks dated. Spend some time browsing Pinterest, magazines, and sales flyers for ideas. Use trendy color palettes, patterns, and styles in your publicity (and follow it through into your décor). Get input from the younger women on your team and in your church.

It can be challenging to find Christian-themed free stock photos. If you can take your own – do it! It is illegal to copy and paste images you find on the internet without obtaining permission. Yes, copyright lawyers really will send you a nasty letter and will threaten to take you to court. You must either purchase images or find free stock images. Be sure to list the source if it is required. Read the fine print and licensing info; that will tell you how you can and cannot use the image. For example, you might not be able to put it on a t-shirt to sell at an event, but it may be okay for you to use on your website. Side note: If you're going to use a close-up photo of your women for publicity purposes, please obtain their permission first. Delete any awkward or unflattering photos.

Outdated publicity sends a clear message to your younger women – this isn't for you.

Good news – it's getting easier and easier to create your own social media graphics and publicity materials! Many websites and apps offer a wide assortment of templates that you can quickly customize to best suit your needs. Do an online search for "graphic design tools" to discover the latest free and paid options.

As you research options, consider:

- Is it free, or are there additional costs? Sometimes it's worth paying the monthly or annual fee to unlock other features.

- Do they offer templates, and if so, what kind?
- Do they offer cloud storage for your creations?
- Do you want to be able to design on the go? Is there an app for that?
- What format do you need for your creation? Hint: Saving as a PNG file results in a cleaner font than saving as a JPG.
- Can you upload and use your own fonts?

If this is outside of your comfort zone, don't panic! Ask for help. Most apps and websites offer tutorials to help you learn how to use their tools. You can also find many helpful videos on YouTube. It's worth pushing yourself over the learning curve!

Videos are wildly popular and almost always get more views on social media channels. Videos are the perfect vehicle for telling a story, and they show and tell women why they should attend. You can also share a behind-the-scenes sneak peek, ask your speaker to create a video for your women before the event, or create a slide show of photos and video of your retreat location. Keep the camera rolling at the event and record testimonies to use in next year's publicity pieces. Take the time to use a microphone or film in a quiet place. Add lighting if needed. There are many apps and tools you can use to edit your footage. Ask for help from some of the younger women and others with technology skills with this piece.

Even as the numbers of social media users rise, the most effective way to reach the majority of women is email.

Even as the numbers of social media users rise, the most effective way to reach the majority of women is email. Many churches have invested in software programs that can allow you to email a segment of church attendees. You may just need to ask if you can have access. If that isn't an option, you may need to build your own email list. There are several online email services you can use for free with up to a certain number of subscribers. Ask women at every function to fill out an information card and include a place for them to opt in or opt out of your women's ministry email list.

Texting apps may also be an option your team will want to consider. However, if their cell phone carrier charges for texts, they may opt out.

REACHING WOMEN IN YOUR COMMUNITY

Not every event necessitates publicity outside of your church community, but when it comes to reaching those beyond our church walls, we sometimes struggle with how to get the word out. Here are a few ideas you may want to add to your publicity arsenal.

21 Ways to Publicize Events to the Community

1. Online community event calendars. Submit your event online to local TV and radio stations, newspapers, and parenting magazines. Search the web to find local community event calendars.
2. Tear-off flyers placed on community boards at the grocery store, coffee shop, etc.
3. Distribute flyers or invitation cards through your church preschool.
4. Send Facebook invites to friends, neighbors, and family outside of your church.
5. Place large outdoor banners on the church property near the road for drivers to see.
6. Door hangers.
7. Postcard mailings to your church zip code/new move-ins.
8. Send invitations and flyers to other local churches (great for big-name speakers).
9. Set up a booth at a local fair (distribute water, provide a nursing station for moms).
10. Radio ads. Check to see if your local Christian station will air an ad or announcement for free.
11. Newspaper announcements. See if your newspaper has a weekly religious announcement section.

12. Facebook ads (if your budget allows).
13. Local community magazines.
14. Local community newspapers.
15. TV interviews (local morning or mid-day show).
16. Postcards at local businesses (tap into your church membership and see if they'll put a stack of cards out at their register).
17. Neighborhood newsletters, email lists, message boards, or websites.
18. Yard signs at member's homes and on busy street corners (if allowed).
19. Denominational newsletters (see if your convention or local affiliation will share your event).
20. Posters in store windows of local businesses.
21. Contact past attendees and invite them back (especially for similar or same events).

Women inside of and outside of our church cannot come if they do not know. As technology changes, we'll need to continue to adapt our publicity methods. The time, energy, and effort to reach more women for Christ is worth it!

Prayer

Lord, please help us to be effective in spreading the word about our activities and events. Help us to create publicity that is appealing and accurate. Help us to use technology as a tool to bring more women to You. Amen.

PRAYER POINTS: WHAT IS GOD PROMPTING ME TO MAKE A MATTER OF PRAYER?

PP

_____
_____
_____
_____
_____
_____
_____

ACTION ITEMS: LIST THOSE THINGS UPON WHICH YOU SENSE GOD IS PROMPTING YOU TO TAKE ACTION.

AI

_____
_____
_____
_____
_____
_____
_____

PART 3
Implementing Change

Trust in the Lord with all your heart and lean not on your own understanding; in all your ways submit to him, and he will make your paths straight.
—Proverbs 3:5–6

Chapter 13

Making Changes and Managing Sacred Cows

*Forget the former things; do not dwell on the past. See, I am
doing a new thing! Now it springs up; do you not perceive it? I am
making a way in the wilderness and streams in the wasteland.*
—Isaiah 43:18–19

CHANCES ARE, IN THE PREVIOUS PAGES you've come across some ideas that will require a change in the way you currently administer women's ministry in your church. You may be excited about the potential results of making those changes, but unsure of how best to approach them. You suspect your women's ministry team members may need some time to process and pray. You know these changes are likely to ruffle a few feathers, but you fear you'll encounter some severe backlash. You may wonder, *Should I even bother? Do I want to battle any opposition? Will it be worth it?*

I've wondered those very same things. In this chapter, we'll tackle those very valid concerns. We'll talk about the sacred cows in women's ministry. We'll discern whether or not it's time to let go of a ministry tradition. I'll also share some tips for dealing with opposition.

IS IT TIME TO KILL A SACRED COW?

What exactly is a sacred cow? Thom S. Rainer describes *sacred cows* as a term "commonly used in churches to describe those facets of church life that are given undue (and sometimes unbiblical) respect to the point they cannot be changed."[46] According to the online Merriam-Webster dictionary, sacred cows are also those traditions, habits, preferences, or ideas that are "often unreasonably immune from criticism or opposition."[47]

Common sacred cows in women's ministry include:

- Annual table events
- Secret sisters
- Retreat locations
- Unspoken dress codes
- Event schedules
- Holiday parties
- Long-held traditions
- Furniture arrangements

New church members are often unaware of sacred cows until they innocently suggest their removal. As we talked through some changes for our new Bible study session, my suggestion to use a couple of Sunday school rooms for the discussion group portion was met with confusion. There wasn't room to set up tables in those spaces. I didn't immediately understand why that was a problem, as I had spent years attending Bible Study Fellowship (BSF) where we had always sat in a circle of chairs and held our materials on our laps. The women in this church always sat at tables for Bible study.

One of our group facilitators wanted to use a room with tables, and the other agreed to try a room without tables but was skeptical it would work. It did work, but for many of our women, it was a bit of an adjustment. It took them time to appreciate the privacy and lack of disruption that was offered by using those rooms instead. Be warned: just because you don't view something as a sacred cow doesn't mean your ladies don't!

> *Be warned: just because you don't view something as a sacred cow doesn't mean your ladies don't!*

Sometimes the need for change is obvious, and sometimes it isn't. Here are some signs it's time for a change:

- Attendance has fallen for this event or activity – either as a whole or by age group.
- The event follows the same schedule (maybe even the same speaker) year after year after year.
- The enthusiasm for this event has started to wane.
- The focus on the event is on something other than Jesus and God's Word.
- The event or activity no longer aligns with your women's ministry mission statement and the church's mission.
- The event fails to draw in new women from inside of and outside of the church.
- The same woman continues to coordinate this event year after year after year.

Eliminating a tradition, especially one that has become what some might call a sacred cow, can cause serious division. It's, unfortunately, something I have experience with.

Before Making a Change or Killing a Sacred Cow

If you feel it's time to bring an end to a beloved women's ministry tradition, or you sense God's leading to kill a sacred cow, before doing anything, spend time in prayer over this decision. You must be confident that the Lord is bringing this event or activity to an end. Write down why you feel this is the direction the team should go so you are prepared to articulate your decision.

Don't be a lone ranger. Changes need to be a team decision, or your ministry could be negatively impacted. If you feel confident this is an event or activity that does not serve the purposes of your women's ministry, take the time to help your team reach that same conclusion. Have your team complete the worksheet titled "Ministry Health Assessment" or use the "Post-Event Evaluation Form." (Both are included in the free bonus materials online.)

Speak with your supervising pastor. You want their input and their backing. Women who disagree with the change your team has made might take their complaints straight to the top. Some pastors may even use their authority to press pause on the event, which removes some of the blame from you and your team. Depending on the situation, you may wish to speak with your pastor before bringing the issue before your team, and vice versa.

Once your team and pastor are on board, it's time to share that vision with other women. Reach out to those with the greatest influence and spend time addressing any of their concerns. You may find they are excited about the new direction in which God is leading!

How Evaluations Can Encourage Change

Change that comes from a team decision, instead of led by a singular person, is often better received. You're able to skip over the step of getting your team on board with the idea. Constant evaluation of events and activities will lead your team to identify areas where change would be beneficial.

When you sit down to work on your calendar for the year (or half-year), take the opportunity to examine every event or activity before it is placed on the calendar.

Ask your team these three questions:

1. Does it need to be refined?
2. Should it be removed?
3. Is it something that should remain?

But how do you decide if it should remain, be removed, or be refined? Once you've begun filling out a post-event evaluation, you'll likely have a good handle on answering those questions. Please know I am not recommending that you go back and fill one of those out for every event or activity you have completed in the past year. That's way too much work! Instead, ask your team these questions:

- Does it meet a need?
- Does it encourage spiritual growth?
- Does it allow opportunities for outreach and service?

- Are you sharing the gospel?
- Is it open to visitors and the community?
- Is it relevant, or has it become outdated?
- Are you reaching multiple age groups?
- Is it tired?
- Does it need refreshing or repackaging?
- Should it be shelved for a year or two so that something new can be tried?
- Is your calendar too full?

Admittedly, removing an event sounds a lot like a root canal without Novocain, but it doesn't have to be. It is better to remove a popular program while it's still popular rather than waiting until it isn't. Focus on ending on a high note rather than risk losing women over time. When removing an activity or event, be sure to have a replacement ready – unless your calendar is too crowded.

God may lead you to refine your event instead of to remove it. It's also possible that reworking the event or activity could prevent the need to permanently remove it. I've mentioned the annual table event before, and now it's time to tell you the rest of the story. That event was identified as a sacred cow. Pulling the plug abruptly on this beloved event would likely have resulted in a revolt, so the team implemented two changes the next year to direct the focus from the décor to the message.

God may lead you to refine your event instead of to remove it.

First, we changed the order and location of the message. The event began with our message in the sanctuary, instead of the fellowship hall where the tables were set up. You probably won't be surprised to hear that didn't go as well as I had hoped! Women wanted to see the tables, despite our signs on the doors, greeters at the entrance, and directions in our publicity materials. Several women tried to enter through the back door so they could walk through the fellowship hall before heading to the sanctuary. Frustrated that women were ignoring our directions, at one point, I physically locked the back door, but our men who were serving needed access. Thankfully, these women were the exception and not the norm.

Our second change, as I mentioned in the chapter on mentoring and discipleship, was to include a speaker that would draw in our younger women. Attendance in years past was significantly skewed to the fifties and older crowd, which led most of our younger women to believe this event was not for them. Our youngest speaker that night was well-known and much-loved by the younger women in our church. Her friends were excited to show up to hear her speak. Success!

If God's leading you down the path of refining:

- Seek input from across the generations.
- Update when possible – fresh graphics, new theme, use technology, etc.
- Add a service or outreach component.
- Change up the order. (For example, start with the speaker and end with dinner.)
- Change the day, time, schedule, length, or location.
- Add depth.
- Remove anything unnecessary.
- Keep the meat – don't skimp on the message.

Try making a change before giving an event the ax. Change the schedule, change the location, or change the emphasis. Don't change *everything* at once. Make incremental changes over several years, until the event becomes what you feel God is leading it to be.

Consider hosting the event in alternating years. This can be especially beneficial if the event or activity is a drain on the women's ministry budget. When women see what else can be done with those funds, they might not hold on so tightly.

Make every tweak, adjustment, or change a matter of prayer. God's timing and His will for your church and your women are most important. We may be ready for change, but it may not yet be God's timing.

How Not to Kill a Sacred Cow

Several years ago, I tried to bring an abrupt end to a program called Secret Sisters at a church in which I served. For many years, a small number (twenty to thirty out of five hundred) of mostly women above age sixty in our church participated in a secret sister program. They would purchase small gifts and send cards to their secret sister for most of a year. In the spring, there was always a big reveal luncheon or brunch for the group who had participated.

I believed we needed to eliminate the secret sister program because:

- The budget for the reveal brunch ($300) was more than the line item for events that were for *all* of the women in the church.
- Women could only join once a year, which excluded anyone new from participating.
- Some participants failed to participate – you could show love to your secret sister but receive nothing in return. The risk of hurt feelings was high.
- Our younger women were not interested in the program (we were focused on increasing their participation).
- It was inward focused, rather than outward focused.

It's been many years, so some of the details are fuzzy, but I do recall that I didn't do enough to address my concerns before omitting the program from the budget proposal. I failed to follow the previously mentioned steps and suffered the consequences.

When I explained my concerns to the team, emphasizing that I did not feel $300 on an event that only about twenty women participated in was in line with the rest of our budget, a couple of team members were quick to find ways to cut the cost of the reveal luncheon. In the end, they decided to charge each woman $10 for brunch, and it was decided we would draft a letter (to be reviewed and approved by our pastor) to all of the participants letting them know we would be suspending the secret sister program. It was a difficult meeting, and I left feeling like I had made some enemies that day. The luncheon went on as planned, minus the $300 price tag, and we pressed pause on Secret

Sisters for the next year. It was the right decision, but I went about it all wrong. I pray you won't do the same!

TIPS FOR DEALING WITH OPPOSITION

There's a very strong possibility that you'll encounter opposition with any changes you make. Expect pushback. Some of your women won't like anyone messing with an event, tradition, or element they dearly love. It may feel as if those against change far outnumber those who are for the change, but feelings can be deceiving. Carey Nieuwhof, in his book, *Leading Change Without Losing It,* breaks down the opposition into four categories:

> 10% are opposed and loud
> 10% are audibly enthusiastic
> 30% are inaudibly supportive
> 50% are quietly neutral to hopeful

Despite how it may seem, that means 90% "either will be or are already in favor of change."[48] We cannot let that loud 10% keep our ministry from moving forward. Our task is to focus on the 90% (including those women who are not coming yet) that will benefit from the changes we are making. A simple "thank you for sharing your concerns" may be enough to appease some of your women who are vocally opposed to the changes. It can be helpful to explain the reasoning behind the changes at your fall kick-off or start to Bible study. For example:

"We're excited about how this change will allow working women in our church to participate."

"Our team has been praying about how we can better reach out to women in the community, and we're excited to add more opportunities for outreach on our women's ministry calendar this year."

I have to be very careful when I am confident in God's leading that I don't bulldoze the nay-sayers. To keep myself from saying things I'll have to apologize for later, I have a twenty-four hour rule. I make myself wait for twenty-four hours before I respond to criticism. Usually, that's enough time for me to work through my emotions and reply in a more Christ-like manner. My husband is also a great sounding board, and I almost always ask him to read any written communication before I send it. Writing also helps me to work through my thoughts. I never enter an email address when I'm typing up an email though, as I know there's always the chance I will hit the wrong button and send it accidentally.

Some women may decide that rather than adapt to the changes you and your team have made, they will stop participating. Try not to take it personally. It really is their loss. Sometimes God will remove the opposition so the ministry can move forward. I know that sounds harsh and not very sympathetic, but I've been the recipient of such an event. You may remember the MOPS team I mentioned in an earlier chapter; after that first tumultuous year, we had to rebuild our team from the ground up. I cried buckets of tears for weeks, and were it not for God's crystal-clear calling and scriptural confirmation I would have walked away. Obedience amid change can be hard.

Obedience amid change can be hard.

Is It Worth It?

Yes! Absolutely, yes! Not only will God grow and refine your faith in Him, but change can provide the opportunity to reach women who are not coming. Let's bring into the game those women that are sitting on the sidelines observing! Let's invite them to live a life where Jesus is everything! Consider what will happen if you don't make the changes God has prompted you or your team to make. Are those consequences you can live with?

○ ○ ○ ○ ○

Prayer

Lord, give us discernment when it comes to events that are a tradition in our women's ministry. Help us to know when we've strayed from Your purpose. Give us the insight to make any necessary changes. Prepare the hearts of our women as we seek to do Your will. Amen

PRAYER POINTS: WHAT IS GOD PROMPTING ME TO MAKE A MATTER OF PRAYER?

PP

_____
_____
_____
_____
_____
_____
_____

ACTION ITEMS: LIST THOSE THINGS UPON WHICH YOU SENSE GOD IS PROMPTING YOU TO TAKE ACTION.

AI

_____
_____
_____
_____
_____
_____
_____

Chapter 14

Final Thoughts

THOUGHT I HAD A SOLID HANDLE on women's ministry terminology and programming until I began to write this book. As I've worked on each chapter, God challenged me to dig into the why behind my beliefs.

Does Scripture support my thought process?

Is there a better way to do what we've been doing?

Is this what's best for our women?

Are my assumptions accurate and true?

Are my decisions driven by tradition?

Who are we failing to reach?

I hope this book has challenged some of your beliefs, definitions, and assumptions about women's ministry too. I pray you'll be open to rethinking some of the ways you've traditionally implemented women's ministry so you can better reach the women in your church and community.

Your women, your church, and your situation are unique. The ideas on these pages may need some tweaking to work best in your situation. I pray God will guide your application and that He alone will be glorified.

Gather and glean as the Lord leads.

Be attentive to the Holy Spirit.

Pay attention to the places where your heart bristled. It can be tempting to skip over those ideas that make you uncomfortable, but they may just be where God is getting ready to do some of His best work!

Women's ministry can be hard, and it can be complicated, but it is absolutely worth it. Francis Chan, in *Letters to the Church,* points out the church's "purpose is not just to exist. It's to produce. Are we producing mature disciples who imitate Christ by constantly serving others? Are we developing communities that are so deeply in love with one another that the world marvels (John 13:34–35)?"[49]

Lord, help us to cultivate flourishing communities that deeply love one another. Show us how to encourage the spiritual growth of our women. Direct our steps and give us discernment in how best to serve and love the women You place in our path. May You receive all the glory! Amen.

God bless you and your ministry,

Cyndee

Acknowledgements

I thank God for ignoring the prayers over twenty years ago of this (then) young Christian to "send someone to lead our women's ministry team because I know it isn't me." I am absolutely humbled that the Lord would use me, the girl who struggled to make friends with other girls in school, to serve on multiple women's ministry teams. Thank you for giving me the opportunity to encourage other leaders; it is an honor and it gives me such joy!

To my husband, Sean, and our two boys, Nick and Cameron, thank you for enduring months of thrown-together meals and an extra-messy home when big ministry projects took precedence over housework. I love you all more than words can say, but God loves you even more. Sean, thank you for supporting and encouraging me through the years as I've served countless hours leading Bible studies and planning women's ministry events. I'm blessed to have you listen and advise me.

Mom, you have always been my biggest cheerleader. Thank you for listening as I rambled on and on about women's ministry over the years. Thank you for all those times you've let me vent and for those yet to come. I am so thankful to have you in my corner. I think Dad would be proud.

To my sisters, Kristy and Katy, and the Ownbeys, your prayers and support over the years mean more than you'll ever know. Thank you for living out Psalm 145:4.

To Kim Powell, who mentored me from MOPS into women's ministry, thank you for teaching me how to pray out loud and how to seek scriptural confirmation. You are a living example of Titus 2. I am so thankful for you and the rest of our prayer group, Becki, Lois, and Susan.

To all the women I've had the awesome opportunity to serve alongside these past twenty years, thank you for the grace you extended when I made mistakes – there were plenty! Thank you for praying with me and for me as we tried to figure out how best to "do" women's ministry. May God continue to bless your efforts for His kingdom.

To my beta reader team – Anna, Beverly, Brandi, Debbie, Donna, Jenni, JoAnn, Jana, Katie, Kristi, Linda, Leslie, Patty, and Penny – I am forever grateful for your feedback and support. Your input made this book better. Thank you for giving so unselfishly of your time.

To Michelle Rayburn, my book designer and copy editor, thank you for creating something beautiful with my words!

To my Women's Ministry Toolbox readers and Facebook group members, there would not be a book without you! Little did I know when I launched my little website in the spring of 2013 how God would allow me to connect with thousands of leaders around the world. It has been my pleasure to provide you with resources for the work you do in your church. Thank you for your support!

And to you, the reader and women's ministry leader, thank you for picking up this book and opening your heart and mind to "doing" women's ministry a bit differently. God sees your hard work and knows how much you love the women in your church and community. Don't give up when the work becomes difficult. It is worth it. He is with you and He will guide you. Seek His will above all else. May the Lord grant you wisdom and discernment as you seek to point more women to Him.

About the Author

Cyndee Ownbey is a mentor to thousands of women's ministry leaders through her website and Facebook community, Women's Ministry Toolbox. Pulling from twenty years of experience with ministering to women, Cyndee shares tried-and-true women's ministry tips and ideas while pointing leaders toward God and the Holy Word. Service in women's ministries in five different churches enables Cyndee to relate to a variety of ministry situations and challenges.

Over the years, God has expanded the reach of Women's Ministry Toolbox to include a Facebook group of over 3000 women's ministry leaders, an online classroom featuring women's ministry training, and several printable women's ministry resources. In the fall of 2019, Cyndee launched the first Gather and Glean Women's Ministry Training and Retreat for leaders to gather and glean inspiration IRL from one another.

Cyndee's resources for leaders include:

- READ Bible Study Workbook and Group Kit
- Prayer Warrior Boot Camp Online Course and Group Kit
- Bible Study Facilitator Training Online Course
- Women's Ministry Event Planning Online Course
- How to Select a Bible Study for Your Group Online Course
- *Women's Ministry Binder Essentials* eBook
- *Everything You Need to Know About Planning a Retreat* eBook
- *12 Days of Christmas Icebreaker Games* eBook

FOR MORE INFORMATION VISIT:
womensministrytoolbox.com/resources

Cyndee enjoys training women's ministry leaders and teaching at women's events and conferences when the opportunity allows.

When she isn't serving in the church as a Bible study leader or encouraging leaders online, you'll likely find Cyndee curled up with a good book. Cyndee and her husband enjoy cheering for the Tarheels and spending time with their sons at the beach.

You can find her on Facebook, Instagram, and Pinterest **@womensministrytoolbox** and online at **www.womensministrytoolbox.com**

Recommended Resources

Chapter 1 – Who Are We Trying to Reach?
Books
> *The Passion Generation: The Seemingly Reckless, Definitely Disruptive, But Far From Hopeless Millennials* by Grant Skeldon with Ryan Casey Waller
> *The Millennials: Connecting to America's Largest Generation* by Thom S. Rainer and Jess Rainer
> *Gen Z: The Culture, Beliefs, and Motivations Shaping the Next Generation* by Barna Group

Chapter 2 – Impact of Social Media and the Internet
Website links
> DivorceCare - **www.divorcecare.org**
> Celebrate Recovery - **www.celebraterecovery.com**

Chapter 3 – Community and Cliques
Website links
> Icebreakers and Games - **womensministrytoolbox.com/icebreakers-games**

Chapter 5- Rethinking Meetings
Books
> *Leading Women Who Wound: Strategies for an Effective Ministry* by Sue Edwards and Kelley Matthews

Printable Materials
> Women's Ministry Binder Essentials – **www.womensministrytoolbox.com/womens-ministry-binder-essentials**

Chapter 6 – Rethinking Bible Study

Online Course

    Bible Study Facilitator Training – **www.bsftraining.com**

Printable Materials

    READ Bible Study – **www.readbiblestudy.com**

Chapter 7 – Rethinking Testimonials and Devotionals

Evangelism Tools

    Life in Six Words – **lifein6words.com**

    One Verse Evangelism from the Navigators –

        www.navigators.org/resource/one-verse-evangelism

    The Bridge to Life from the Navigators –

        www.navigators.org/resource/the-bridge-to-life

Books

    Sharing Jesus Without Freaking Out: Evangelism the
        Way You Were Born to Do It by Alvin Reid

    Tell Someone: You Can Share the Good News by Greg Laurie

Chapter 8 – Rethinking Mentoring and Discipleship

Books

    Adorned: Living Out the Beauty of the Gospel
        Together by Nancy DeMoss Wolgemuth

    Disciple Her: Using the Word, Work & Wonder of
        God to Invest in Women by Kandi Gallaty

    Giddy, Up Eunice: Because Women Need
        Each Other by Sophie Hudson

    MARCS of a Disciple: A Biblical Guide for Gauging
        Spiritual Growth by Robby Gallaty

    Mentoring for All Seasons: Sharing Life Experiences
        and God's Faithfulness by Janet Thompson

Printable Materials

    Prayer Warrior Boot Camp for Groups

        www.prayerwarriorbootcamp.com

    READ Bible Study Kit for Groups **www.readbiblestudy.com**

Chapter 9 – Service Projects and Missions

Website links

Blessing Bags: **womensministrytoolbox.com/ encouragement-blessing-bags**

Habitat for Humanity: **habitat.org**

Meals on Wheels: **mealsonwheelsamerica.org**

No-sew Fleece Blankets: **womensministrytoolbox.com/ local-mission-project-idea-no-sew-fleece-blankets**

Operation Christmas Child: **samaritanspurse.org/ operation-christmas-child/pack-a-shoe-box**

SoleHope: **solehope.org**

The Sonshine Box: **womensministry- toolbox.com/sonshine-box**

Books

When Helping Hurts: How to Alleviate Poverty without Hurting the Poor...and Yourself by Steve Corbett and Brian Fikkert

Bonus Materials

You'll find the worksheets, forms, and assessments mentioned throughout *Rethinking Women's Ministry* available as a free downloadable PDF at **www.rethinkingwomensministry.com.**

- 31 Introduction Icebreaker Questions
- Bible Study Habits
- Discussion Group Guidelines
- Post Event Evaluation Form
- Publicity Form
- Share Your God Story
- Women's Ministry Health Assessment
- Women's Ministry Team Covenant
- Women's Ministry Team Needs Assessment

Notes

1 2018 Women's Ministry Survey conducted by Cyndee Ownbey, August 8, 2018–September 7, 2018, via Survey Monkey. Statistics and results available at Women's Ministry Toolbox.

    Part 1: www.womensministrytoolbox.com/part-1-survey-results

    Part 2: www.womensministrytoolbox.com/part-2-womens-ministry-survey-statistics

    Part 3: www.womensministrytoolbox.com/part-3-womens-ministry-survey-comments

2 Thom S. Rainer and Jess W. Rainer, *The Millennials: Connecting to America's Largest Generation.* (Nashville: B&H Publishing, 2011), 3, 35, 41, 47, 57, 66, 69, 104, 259.

3 Barna Group and Impact 360 Institute, *Gen Z: The Culture, Beliefs, and Motivations Shaping the Next Generation.* (Barna Group, 2018), 12-16, 19, 25, 104.

4 Barna Group and Impact 360 Institute, *Gen Z*, 107.

5 Mark DeWolf, "12 Stats About Working Women," U.S. Department of Labor (blog), March 1, 2017, https://blog.dol.gov/2017/03/01/12-stats-about-working-women/.

6 DeWolf, "12 Stats About Working Women."

7 Thom S. Rainer, "Five Reasons Church Members Attend Less Frequently." Thom S. Rainer (blog), May 22, 2017, https://thomrainer.com/2017/05/five-reasons-church-members-attend-church-less-frequently/.

8 Barna Group and Impact 360 Institute, *Gen Z, 25.*

9 "LifeWay Research: Americans Are Fond of the Bible, Don't Actually Read It." *LifeWay Research*, April 25, 2017, https://lifewayresearch.com/2017/04/25/lifeway-research-americans-are-fond-of-the-bible-dont-actually-read-it/.

10   "Time Flies: U.S. Adults Now Spend Nearly Half a Day Interacting With Media," Nielsen, July 31, 2018, https://www.nielsen.com/us/en/insights/article/2018/time-flies-us-adults-now-spend-nearly-half-a-day-interacting-with-media/.

11   Sammy Nickalls, "Infographic: Women Use Their Phones for Way More Than Just Communicating," *Adweek*, April 8, 2018, https://www.adweek.com/digital/infographic-women-use-their-phones-for-way-more-than-communicating/.

12   Rheana Murray, "Social Media Is Affecting the Way We View Our Bodies — And It's Not Good," *Today*, May 8, 2018, https://www.today.com/style/social-media-affecting-way-we-view-our-bodies-it-s-t128500/.

13   Murray, "Social Media Is Affecting the Way We View Our Bodies — And It's Not Good."

14   Aaron Smith and Monica Anderson, "Social Media Use in 2018," Pew Research Center, March 1, 2018, https://www.pewinternet.org/2018/03/01/social-media-use-in-2018/.

15   Craig Groeschel, *#Struggles: Following Jesus in a Selfie-Centered World* (Grand Rapids: Zondervan, 2015), 79.

16   Oxford English Dictionary, "clique", accessed July 10, 2019, https://www.lexico.com/en/definition/clique/.

17   Robby Gallaty, *MARCS of a Disciple: A Biblical Guide for Gauging Spiritual Growth* (Hendersonville: Replicate Ministries, 2016), 26.

18   Sophie Hudson, *Giddy Up, Eunice: Because Women Need Each Other* (Nashville: B&H Publishing, 2016), 30.

19   Thom S. Rainer, *Becoming a Welcoming Church* (Nashville: B&H Publishing Group, 2018), 2-3.

20   Rainer, *Welcoming Church*, 8.

21   Sue Edwards and Kelley Matthews, *Leading Women Who Wound: Strategies for an Effective Ministry* (Chicago IL: Moody Publishers, 2009), 73.

22   Francis Chan, *Letters to the Church* (Colorado Springs: David C. Cook, 2018), 91.

23   Eric Geiger, "5 Truths About Great Ministry Leaders," Eric Geiger (blog), January 5, 2017, https://ericgeiger.com/2017/01/5-truths-about-great-ministry-leaders/.

24 Edwards and Matthews, *Leading Women Who Wound*, 12-13.

25 Edwards and Matthews, *Leading Women Who Wound*, 136.

26 Barna Group, *Barna Trends 2017: What's New and What's Next at the Intersection of Faith and Culture* (Grand Rapids: Baker Books, 2016), 138.

27 Jen Wilkin, *Women of the Word: How to Study the Bible with Both Our Hearts and Our Mind* (Wheaton, IL: Crossway, 2014).

28 Francis Chan, *Letters to the Church* (Colorado Springs: David C. Cook, 2018).

29 Wilkin, *Women of the Word*, 45.

30 Wilkin, *Women of the Word*, 36.

31 Donald S. Whitney, *Spiritual Disciplines for the Christian Life* (Colorado Springs: NavPress, 1991), 106.

32 Nancy De Moss Wolgemuth, *Adorned: Living Out the Beauty of the Gospel Together* (Chicago: Moody Publishers, 2017), 79.

33 Whitney, *Spiritual Disciplines*, 111.

34 Wolgemuth, *Adorned*, 61.

35 Kandi Gallaty, *Disciple Her: Using the Word, Work, & Wonder of God to Invest in Women* (Nashville: B&H Publishing, 2019), 32.

36 Janet Thompson, *Mentoring for All Seasons: Sharing Life Experiences and God's Faithfulness* (Abilene, TX: Leafwood Publishers, 2017), 42.

37 Gallaty, *MARCS of a Disciple*, xx.

38 Thompson, *Mentoring for All Seasons*, 49.

39 Wolgemuth, *Adorned*, 75.

40 Grant Skeldon, *The Passion Generation: The Seemingly Reckless, Definitely Disruptive, But Far From Hopeless Millennials* (Grand Rapids, MI: Zondervan, 2018), 197.

41 Amy Lively, *How to Love Your Neighbor without Being Weird* (Bloomington, MN: Bethany House, 2015), 39.

42 Gallaty, *MARCS of a Disciple*, 14-15.

43 Steven Corbett and Brian Fikkert, *When Helping Hurts: How to Alleviate Poverty without Hurting the Poor...and Yourself* (Chicago: Moody Publishers, 2012), 27.

44 Corbett and Fikkert, *When Helping Hurts*, 99.

45 Kathi Kruse, "Rule of 7: How Social Media Crushes Old School Marketing." *Kruse Control* (blog), March 29, 2018, https://www.krusecontrolinc.com/rule-of-7-how-social-media-crushes-old-school-marketing/.

46 Thom S. Rainer, "15 Common Sacred Cows in Churches." Thom S. Rainer (blog), August 27, 2018, https://thomrainer.com/2018/08/15-common-sacred-cows-churches/.

47 Merriam-Webster, "sacred cows," accessed July 24, 2019, https://www.merriam-webster.com/dictionary/sacred%20cow/.

48 Carey Nieuwhof, *Leading Change Without Losing It: Five Strategies That Can Revolutionize How You Lead Change When Facing Opposition* (Cumming, GA: The reThink Group, Inc., 2012), 43.

49 Chan, *Letters to the Church*, 93.

Made in the USA
Columbia, SC
21 October 2021